BARTON CREEK

RIVER BOOKS
Sponsored by

Andrew Sansom, General Editor

BARTON CREEK

ED CROWELL

Photographs by Alberto Martinez
Foreword by Andrew Sansom

Copyright © 2019 by Ed Crowell
All rights reserved
First edition

This paper meets the requirements
of ANSI/NISO Z39.48–1992 (Permanence of Paper).
Binding materials have been chosen for durability.
Manufactured in China through FCI Print Group.

LIBRARY OF CONGRESS CATALOGING-IN-PUBLICATION DATA

Names: Crowell, Ed, 1948– author. | Sansom, Andrew, writer of foreword.
Title: Barton Creek / Ed Crowell; photographs by Alberto Martinez; foreword by Andrew Sansom.
Description: First edition. | College Station: Texas A&M University Press,
  [2019] | Series: River Books | Includes bibliographical references and index. |
Identifiers: LCCN 2018033736 (print) | LCCN 2018055278 (ebook) | ISBN 9781623497309 (ebook) | ISBN 9781623497293 | ISBN 9781623497293 (flex with flaps: alk. paper)
Subjects: LCSH: Barton Creek (Hayes County and Travis County, Tex.)—Environmental conditions. | Springs—Texas—Texas Hill Country—Environmental conditions. | Spring ecology—Texas—Texas Hill Country. | Environmental protection—Texas—Austin—Citizen participation. | Water conservation—Texas—Austin.
Classification: LCC TD171.3.T42 (ebook) | LCC TD171.3.T42 T493 2019 (print) | DDC 333.91/620976431—dc23
LC record available at https://lccn.loc.gov/2018033736

*To my grandchildren,
Gabriella, Judson, Charlotte, and Sunny,
all lovers of the natural world*

CONTENTS

Foreword, by Andrew Sansom ... ix

Acknowledgments ... xi

    Introduction ... 1

1. **The End:** *A Bustling Cityscape Where an Aquifer's Springs Fill a Historic Pool* ... 3
2. **Saving Salamanders:** *Searching For, Counting, and Raising Two Endangered Species* ... 14
3. **Family Lands:** *The Starks' Summer Camp and the Family Legacy of Truman Breed* ... 24
4. **Public Battles:** *Barton Springs Uprising Stokes Decades of Political and Legal Fights* ... 34
5. **Shield Ranch:** *Six Miles and Sixty-Eight Hundred Acres of Protected Water and Land* ... 44
6. **Wild Greenbelt:** *Pleasures, Dangers, and Challenges in Canyons above Barton Springs* ... 55
7. **Hidden Neighbors:** *Famed Author's Retreat and The Nature Conservancy's Preserve* ... 65
8. **Vireos and Warblers:** *Working to Keep Thousands of Acres of Habitat Beckoning Birds* ... 73
9. **Checking for Pollutants:** *Watershed Checkups amid New Pressures from Development* ... 83
10. **Generations of Care:** *Rancher Henry Brooks and the Puryears Protect Their Lands* ... 93
11. **Conserving History:** *Reviewing an Easement Where an 1800s Pioneer Era Ended* ... 105
12. **The Beginning:** *Ralph Roy Breed's Pasture Trickle and a Farm for Cheesemaking* ... 113

Further Reading and Resources ... 121

Index ... 123

FOREWORD

I came to Austin in 1982 to work for The Nature Conservancy. There really wasn't much to the organization at that time, and we seemed to perpetually teeter on the brink of insolvency. Ironically, though we were located in the most progressive city in Texas, few of the donors we depended on lived in the state's capital, and we had few prospects. The lack of support in Austin became even more obvious as we attempted to finance protection of rare properties elsewhere in the state, including in the meadows of the Blackland Prairie, the marshes along the coast, and the mountains of the Trans-Pecos. Austin's disinterest in our work was so bad we decided to move the organization to San Antonio, where we had initiated a big project and where ties to the rural landscape of Texas were stronger.

But things began to change in Austin when the treasured swimming hole at the mouth of Barton Creek became more and more threatened by runoff from land increasingly covered with cement and asphalt, pollution from leaking sewer lines, and contamination from fertilizers and pesticides used to groom lawns in the growing metropolitan area surrounding the creek.

Faced with repeated closures of the Barton Springs Pool, activists in Austin staged a virtual uprising. As Ed Crowell recounts in the twenty-fifth volume of the series *River Books*, published through the partnership of Texas A&M University Press and The Meadows Center for Water and the Environment at Texas State University, the confrontations were ugly and included angry litigation, all night city council meetings, a documentary featuring the actor Robert Redford, and more.

Out of the chaos, an organization called Save Our Springs was born. Under the leadership of lawyer Bill Bunch and activist Brigid Shea and with supporters like Kirk Mitchell and others, Austin began to wake up and face not only the mounting threats to Barton Springs but also the multiple environmental dangers resulting from rapid growth to the entire region and beyond.

Today, largely thanks to the tumultuous beginnings of SOS, as the organization is commonly known, Austin, along with Travis County, Hays County, the City of San Antonio, and Bexar County, have spent more money protecting resources like the Barton Creek watershed, the recharge zone of the Edwards Aquifer, and habitat for endangered species than the entire state and federal government combined have spent in Texas. The Nature Conservancy has played a major role in this monumental effort, helping to generate more than $1 billion in funding for land conservation along the Interstate 35 corridor.

Thus, for the moment, Barton Springs has more protection than ever before, and, just as important, the fight to save the pool has spawned many other efforts to preserve the best of the Texas Hill Country, including its numerous iconic springs. And The Nature Conservancy has moved back to Austin.

ACKNOWLEDGMENTS

Michael Adams for his dedication to writers and their sojourns at Paisano

Austin History Center staff for their generous research assistance

Michael Barnes for his high-energy model of interviewing and writing

J. Marie Bassett for her knowledge of Hays County history

Brandon Crawford for protecting an island of green for The Nature Conservancy

Margie Crisp for pointing the way with her Colorado River book

Frank Davis and Jeff Francell for their land-conservation efforts and successes

Tom Devitt and Donnelle Robinson for sharing the springs they protect

Karen Kocher for her ongoing *Living Springs* video documentary series

Bill McCann for thoughtful editing and encouragement

Kate McKenna for a great respite in Mexico's Copper Canyon

Kim McKnight for guidance on local history sources

Christy Muse for her help through Shield Ranch visits

Vance Naumann and Janet Wilson for maps, advice, and listening on the Llano

Asher Price for his excellent reporting and sharing his sources

Gary Rice for hiking company and action scenes advice

Susan and Richard Stark for their welcome and introductions to neighbors

Pete Szilagyi for his friendship and the guidance of his 1982 reporting on Barton Creek

Kevin Thuesen for a tutorial on the Balcones Canyonlands Preserve tracts

Terry Tull for backgrounding me on water issues and a 2005 regional water quality study he led

City of Austin's Watershed Protection Department for so many committed scientists

And especially for . . .

Alberto Martinez, a true friend and artist who makes excellent photos

Lynda Crowell, who made this book and all things possible

BARTON CREEK

INTRODUCTION

Barton Creek is one of the most cherished little creeks in America. Spilling through what once was mostly farms and ranchlands and wooded canyons into the heart of Austin, the creek concludes its journey with powerful natural springs pumping into a massive, treasured city pool. When my family and I moved to Austin from a Florida beach town in the late 1970s, we wanted to be near water and my downtown office. Our house in Barton Hills was close enough to Barton Springs Pool that we could bike or hike there through the neighborhood. Trails down on the creek were too rough, unmarked, and inaccessible. I presumed the land was private. For years, I had no idea where Barton Creek started. Now I know. Searches for the source took me along fifty miles of twists and turns and tributary confluences. Welcoming, proud landowners invited me to see their sections of the stream that range from determined flows past boulders and cliffs to barely a trickle across cow pastures. I swam where the creek sculpts idyllic, shaded holes between meanders.

What's not visible are the passions and scars of political battles to save Barton Springs, Barton Creek, and the Edwards Aquifer below. For decades, those fights embroiled citizen groups, developers, lawyers, city officials, and, in turn, state lawmakers and federal regulators. Some of the battles never ceased and watchdog groups push on. Barton Creek is a success story today. Recent water-quality surveys by city scientists rank it among the healthiest of the forty-nine Austin-area creek watersheds regularly checked for pollutants. It's been years since Barton Springs Pool was closed because of contaminants. Yet upstream threats to the future of the 109-square-mile Barton Creek watershed pop into view as the rooftops and streets of new subdivisions, with signs advertising more to come. Bulldozers scrape roads and homesites into the hills around the former tiny towns of Dripping Springs and Bee Cave. Unseen in full measure so far are the cumulative, polluting components of this development: erosion, runoff from fouled asphalt, fertilizers and pesticides, pet waste, trash, and the effluent of wastewater treatment plants.

What stopped more, earlier developments in the Barton Creek watershed was a determined strategy in the 1990s by city and county voters, environmental partners, and good-hearted property owners. They created a network of thousands of acres of conservation lands protected forever from urbanization. It's an unfinished mosaic that land- and water-protection advocates still try to fill in with new easements and acquisitions through bond issues.

The Barton Springs segment of the Edwards Aquifer lies below Barton Creek and five other area creeks. The sensitive aquifer is a virtual river flowing through honeycombed limestone formations and caverns. Rainwater pours into the aquifer from streambeds, sinkholes, cave openings, and fissures. Unlike in the sand aquifers of other regions, water passes quickly through the Edwards limestone without filtration of pollutants. Springs and seeps bring water up to the creeks, rivers, ponds, and wells. Barton Springs Pool fills with the force of millions of gallons of water per day from one of the strongest sets of springs in Texas.

My journeys to every mile of Barton Creek began at the end, where the creek meets the Colorado River. Barton Springs Pool is just a half mile upstream, a postcard-perfect respite for more than eight hundred thousand visitors a year. How many of them know about the repeated closings of the pool in the 1980s and 1990s because of high pollution counts? The history of Barton Springs includes Native Americans who used the waters for centuries, followed by settlers, grist mills, group baptisms, and a series of bathing concessions and pool-construction projects. Creation of Zilker Park, Austin's equivalent of Central Park, wouldn't have happened without the springs there.

This book is neither an exhaustive history of Barton Creek nor a prelude to an unalterable future. It is a snapshot in time based on two years of personal exploration and learning about the creek from landowners, scientists, and other protectors. Barton Creek and its southern neighbor Onion Creek, a larger contributor to the aquifer, flow with an unsettled urgency today. Newcomers by the thousands are moving to Central Texas atop the fragile Edwards Aquifer that stretches for some 240 miles east from Brackettville and then north to Salado. Wells draw drinking water from the aquifer for small communities and cities as large as San Antonio. Austin's water is pulled from the Colorado River upstream of its confluence with Barton Creek, but the creek contributes to the river's flow for downstream users and benefits its health and ecosystem. Will future populations have the Edwards Aquifer and the region's surface water as reliable sources of clean water?

Endangered birds and salamanders play a huge role in the protections afforded to the watersheds around Austin. An armada of dedicated scientists and city workers oversees water quality in the creeks with frequent inspections and analyses. The property owners I visited who live on or near Barton Creek share my concerns about the celebrated stream as new developments close in on them. The Starks and the Breeds opened their gates and told me their tales of life on the creek. I learned about long-ago pioneers and modern land conservation from the Ayreses and the Doerrs. The Brookses and the Sweethardts showed me the fields and herds they work for incomes while protecting the land and riparian areas.

I returned again and again to Barton Springs Pool, where memories were forged with my young family as we watched serious lap swimmers, linked rafts filled with kids and couples, and met hillside hippies who stayed all day in the shade of towering pecans and oaks. We enjoyed the chilly water that flowed from springs in the rocky bottom of the pool. I dove to feel the strong upward currents from the fissures, but I knew little at the time about the rare aquatic salamanders that make their home in the springs. Nor did I appreciate the power of Barton Creek when flooding rains came. I floated with my kids down the swollen creek in what is now a seven-mile-long public greenbelt, not realizing the potential dangers. In 2016, Barton Creek's high water claimed the lives of three people. Most years, slow summertime tubing is the norm.

The crush of area residents and visitors who enjoy Barton Springs Pool and the greenbelt is certain to increase. Austin has grown from some 320,000 people when I got here forty years ago to a metropolitan population of more than two million. Texas now is second only to California in population. Our state's water resources strain from overtapped aquifers, rivers, and reservoirs. The dependability of replenishing rainfall remains in doubt as droughts occur more frequently.

Barton Creek is a window into those deep concerns. It also is a much-loved icon of environmental integrity that should be explored and understood by new and longtime residents alike. There is much to honor with the protections and conservation acreage in place and much to discover as rolling seas of new rooftops and crowded roadways push out to the creek's source. The people who dwell beside the creek or who work to save it shared their stories with me because they passionately want to keep it flowing into the hearts of future generations.

1 🌿 THE END

A Bustling Cityscape Where an Aquifer's Springs Fill a Historic Pool

The very end of Barton Creek, its mouth, reveals little of where it's been. No historical markers. None of the green roadside notices upstream that read "Entering Barton Creek Watershed." No falls, boulders, canyons, or bone-dry sections. No old ranches or gated estates or new sprawling subdivisions. Instead, the little creek that helps define big issues in Austin empties into the Colorado River after a straight-and-lazy, half-mile journey from Barton Springs Pool. On this stretch along the eastern boundary of Zilker Park, the creek is a wide and busy urban scene of people and pets, strollers and paddlers, visitors taking photos and hometowners enjoying one of the city's oldest parks. Despite the crush of warm-weather crowds where Barton Creek concludes its fifty-mile flow across two counties, it doesn't take much mental adjustment to see a pastoral picture here. Unmanicured greenery and overhanging shade trees abound on both sides of the clear, slow-moving water. Balletic swans and raucous geese entertain trail walkers and boaters.

One of the creek's most powerful natural forces can be observed if one looks closely for the final spring site tucked into the woods above the south shore. Sunken Garden, ringed by stone terraces, is fenced and locked up to protect endangered salamanders found there. The outflow of that spring runs down a channel and gushes through a metal grate on the creek bank. On a summer morning in 2017 a week after a heavy rainfall, the water that pushes up from deep in the Edwards Aquifer pours out as if a couple of fire hydrants are open full blast. I'm here once again at this familiar part of the creek below Barton Springs Pool to drift on a kayak with my six-year-old grandson and his fishing pole. I have no expectation he'll catch a whopper amid the bustle. Outside the massive pool's downstream end, enclosed by an eighteen-foot-high dam topped with a chain-link fence, we find plenty of action. Water flows through a spillway in the middle of the dam and from a bypass tunnel along the north side of the pool.

The city charges no admission in this shallow area where dogs are allowed off leash. Crowds of wet canines cavort with their equally energetic and wet owners. They splash together over slippery rock formations and a concrete slab. The water is cool and free. It's been that way for decades in this small, unplanned wading area. But in 2014 Austin police suddenly began enforcing existing rules prohibiting swimming below the dam and letting dogs off leash. They cited increased thefts and complaints of illegal behavior (i.e., drinking) in that part of the creek. The City Council, meanwhile, was told higher levels of bacteria had been found there than in the pool. Howls of protest over the police citations came from dog owners used to leash freedom in the spillway water. A few months later enforcement stopped, and the council decided to allow dogs and swimming again at "Barking Springs." A sign went up warning of possible bacteria dangers. I confess never taking my dog below the dam to sniff and socialize with other dogs. But just downstream is where my family has spent untold hours strolling and feeding ducks and chasing turtles from their sunning logs. I used to jog regularly on the trail here, and the area never lacks for interesting people to observe.

Barton Creek ends at its bustling confluence with the Colorado River.

My grandson and I rent a kayak, and he fishes intently while I paddle slowly toward the Colorado River. The body of water ahead seems immense and daring compared to the placid creek. This is the Texas Colorado, not to be confused with the one that carved out the Grand Canyon in Arizona. It makes sense to me to start this book at the end of Barton Creek and at Barton Springs Pool because it is here that most people experience the iconic and historic waters. If you live in or near Austin, you've probably plunged into the chilly, springs-fed pool at least once. If you're visiting as a tourist or on business, it's a must-see stop. Just the view from the pool's main entrance patio is a stunner.

How did this blue-green oasis nearly a thousand feet long get built in the middle of Texas? The feeling that many swimmers experience here is unlike that at any other city pool. Barton Springs is a sacred sanctuary where you're immersed in nature. The springs are alive, pumping water out like heartbeats. The trees above, the grassy slopes, and the fish and other habitants below produce a gentle euphoria that reminds you: "I'm a living thing, too."

Outside the pool, people find different pleasures while walking downstream to creek's end for views of a gleaming downtown and the broad Colorado River. Along the way, Zilker Park attractions offer a slice of another, comforting era apart from Austin's modern

Dogs and their owners rule the shallow water below Barton Springs Pool.

profile. Just past dogland, the trail passes by an aging playground and the Zilker Zephyr miniature train. The train is a good way to see the park from above the creek while waving to picnickers and strollers along a three-mile ride. The playground's best feature for my kids in the 1970s is still there: an antique Austin fire truck with four skinny tires and an open front seat with a steering wheel to turn.

Next up on the shoreline downstream is the Zilker Park Boat Rentals concession, operated by Howard and Dorothy Barnett since 1969, when they started with nine canoes. Today they stock eighty kayaks, sixty canoes, and fifty-seven stand-up paddleboards. Thanks to the springs in and around the pool, there's always enough water for a paddle in this part of the creek. More than once, however, floods pushed over the pool's dams and washed out boats, equipment, and the rental stand. "The latest was on September 30, 2015, when nineteen thousand cubic feet per second of water came crashing down Barton Creek. We get hit hard about every five years," said Howard Barnett, who told me he got interested in canoeing through the Sierra Club.

On this calm summer day, the creek is filled with sitting boaters and standing paddleboarders as they float downstream. It can be a traffic jam at times, but as Barton Creek flows into the river, the crowd spreads out. Some people paddle toward open-water views, and others follow the river's shoreline. The Colorado ranges from four hundred to twenty-five hundred feet wide on its six-mile journey downtown between Tom Miller Dam and Longhorn Dam. Austinites call the river between the dams a lake—Lady Bird Lake. A series of dams in Austin and to the north impounds the Colorado, which stretches from northwest Texas to the Gulf of Mexico. The river and its dammed lakes provide water supplies, flood management, and recreation.

Heading downstream on the creek, we pass below some of Zilker Park's picnic groves with long concrete tables beneath soaring pecan trees. The creek is eighty feet wide here as we paddle under busy Barton Springs Road. The banks on both sides are filled with a tangle of small trees and undergrowth—the natural means of preventing riparian erosion. Temporary fencing along the hike-and-bike trail that parallels the creek holds a sign noting the area is closed for revegetation of native species.

A hundred yards down from Barton Springs Road the trail splits at an arching, steel-and-wood footbridge over Barton Creek. On this hot August day, boatloads of paddlers wait to cheer on teens jumping from the bridge into the creek some twenty feet below. They begin their descent standing on a railing right above a "No Jumping" sign. Atop a small bluff at the east end of the footbridge is a new "luxury" condominium building called Zilkr on the Park. Presumably the "e" was dropped so no one would mistake the four-story beige building as overnight lodging for Zilker Park. For years, the vacant lot at this site hosted tents with artisans selling their goods.

New buildings this close to the creek are rare. In late 2017, Save Barton Creek Association and Save Our Springs Alliance, battlers for the environment for decades, and other public-advocacy groups mounted a campaign to stop a proposal to build a professional soccer team's stadium on city parkland near the creek's mouth. The team's out-of-state owner soon withdrew that outrageous idea.

The trail that crosses the footbridge is part of the city's 10.5-mile loop around Lady Bird Lake, renamed in 2007 from Town Lake to honor the late Lady Bird Johnson, wife of President Lyndon Johnson. She helped raise money in the early 1970s to build the trail, officially the Ann and Roy Butler Hike-and-Bike Trail, named for a former mayor and his wife. Before that civic project, the shoreline was largely inaccessible.

The Colorado River, Barton Creek, and other creeks have defined Austin as a water city from the beginning. Downtown's original core was surveyed and designed as the final capital of the fledgling

Republic of Texas in 1839 between two small creeks—Shoal and Waller—on the north side of the Colorado. It was difficult then to ford the river to the virtually unsettled south side, where the main attraction was the fresh, cool water flowing into what was called Spring Creek. Fertile land along the creek drew William Barton to plant crops and graze livestock there. Grist mills and the first bridge over the river in 1869 brought many more people to Barton Creek.

At the confluence of today's creek and river, we paddle to shore at a favorite trailside resting spot with an artistic two-level gazebo. This is Lou Neff Point, named for a civic leader who served on the Town Lake Beautification Committee in the 1970s. Don't look for an explanatory plaque about her, though one lists City Council members of the time and another lists the gazebo's designers. Pavers are etched with the names of donors to a renovation of the gazebo in 2006.

Tourists and residents alike flock to the benches and stone terraces of Lou Neff Point for photos and more ephemeral experiences. Plenty of small fish and turtles the size of dinner plates linger close to shore. "Look at that one on the log. It's a red-necked turtle," one observer proclaims to a friend. I hesitate to correct him, but when I tell him it's a red-eared turtle, he seems amused. The point's circular stone gazebo is topped with steel latticework. Look up amid the wisteria vines to see suspended beneath the lattice a small metal sculpture of an eagle, a rattlesnake, and an armadillo. They are not having a peaceful entanglement, which is appropriate given the political battles to protect Barton Creek and its springs.

A rapidly growing downtown skyline reflects Austin's population boom.

Across the river is a dramatic view in stark contrast to the fields of grass in the park and the reflections of trees on the surface of the creek. Austin's ever-growing downtown skyline of concrete, steel, and glass soars above the river's opposite shore. The forest of new towers for condos, offices, and hotel rooms puts a giant, sobering punctuation mark on the end of Barton Creek's journey.

A favorite gimmick of local news outlets when new high-rises get built is to compare the skylines of five or ten years ago with today's. The graceful Texas Capitol Building and the simple lines of the 307-foot University of Texas Tower could once be seen from almost anywhere along the shores of the river, but no more. Now developers and their architects compete for prominence with sharp angles, jutting balconies, and rooftop pools. Construction cranes pop up with as much certainty as the roar of traffic on the city's three downtown bridges over the Colorado. Certain to be visible from Lou Neff Point will be Austin's tallest building, a sixty-two-story tower of apartments and offices on the southwest side of downtown, announced in the summer of 2017.

We return to our kayak and paddle upstream without a catch of the day. Before heading home, Judson and I walk to the main entrance of Barton Springs Pool for a peek at swimmers enjoying the bright morning sun. The three acres of water and hillside green there refresh me every time I think about the city's unstoppable growth. Throughout a history much older than the city itself, the springs have survived as a source of sustenance and pleasure.

Ten thousand years ago, humans left evidence that they knew about these sources of fresh water, game, and useful plants. Stone tools, hunting points, burned rocks, and pot shards have been found near the springs. Later tribes of Native Americans who visited here include the Tonkawas, Lipan Apaches, and Comanches. Spanish explorers arrived in the 1730s with short-lived attempts at establishing missions on the creek. Three missions were referenced in accounts, but no physical artifacts exist.

What's known in more detail is that William Barton, a settler from South Carolina, built a cabin on what was called Spring Creek in 1837. The settlement of Waterloo across the river had just a handful of houses then. He moved his large family to the site from a land grant near Bastrop on the Colorado River, where he had farmed for about ten years. Although Barton had threatening brushes with Indians who frequented the creek, the springs became an attraction for visitors and residents of the growing town. Barton's time on the creek was brief, but he lived to see Waterloo chosen as the Republic of Texas capital in 1939 and

Eliza Spring in 1870 was a pretty and popular picnic spot. (Source: PICA00987, Austin History Center, Austin Public Library)

renamed Austin. He died of natural causes in 1840. His eldest son was elected the first sheriff of Austin that year and continued to live at the springs for several years on what became known as Barton's Creek.

Over the next half century, the creek and adjoining parcels of land were owned and occupied by members of the Rabb family. They raised cattle on acreage that today is Zilker Park and leased the springs for grist mills. Names for the spring sites have varied. Some accounts say William Barton named them for three daughters: Parthenia, Eliza, and Zenobia. But family histories do not confirm all three. The common names today are Main instead of Parthenia for the pool's outlets, Eliza for the spring outside the pool's main entrance, and Sunken Garden for what once was called Zenobia or Old Mill on the south side of Barton Creek. A fourth spring in the creek upstream of the pool is known simply as Upper Spring. Mill operations began in 1870 when Italian-born entrepreneur Michael Paggi moved to Austin and leased the spring site now dubbed Sunken Garden. Paggi also ran the first bathing house for the springs and provided transportation to cross the river via a small iron steamboat.

A *Daily State Journal* newspaper account described the scene in 1871:

> We visited yesterday Barton's Springs immediately opposite the city. In our ramblings along the stream we came across Paggi's Grist Mill, which was doing an extensive business. He has one of the springs dammed up, with the waters escaping through a narrow passage which runs his mill, equal to about five horsepower. Mr. Paggi turns out about five bushels of meal per hour, and has ready sale for all he can grind. The spring is beautiful, being about two hundred feet in circumference and about fifteen feet deep, and (with places) arranged around the spring for visitors, where they can sit around and chat, and look at the beautiful trout playing in the deep clear waters. Mr. Paggi does not allow fishing in the spring, as he is trying to raise them and does not want them molested for the present.

In January 1877, however, Paggi was struggling with erratic rainfall and spring flows. The *Daily Democratic Statesman* reported that what "has so long been the pride of this city . . . has nearly gone dry and that now only a hole of muddy water is to be seen where a boiling, bubbling spring with sufficient volume to turn a mill has roared for ages gone by. . . . But very little rain has fallen in this section in the past six months, and whether the beautiful Barton Spring will resume its past vigor when the rains set in again remains to be seen." It did, of course, rain again and the springs were replenished. And other mills were built on the creek.

Beginning in 1901, the Rabb family sold parcels of their land to Andrew Jackson Zilker, an Austin businessman. He raised livestock but found another use for the springs as a founding member of the Austin Lodge of the Benevolent and Protective Order of Elks. Zilker built a stepped amphitheater around Eliza Spring in 1903 as a gathering and bathing facility for members of the Elks.

After his wife died, Zilker offered in 1917 to donate his land, including the springs, to the Austin School Board. The deal he wanted was for the City Council, in turn, to buy the land for $100,000, turning it into a park and the money funding an education endowment. City voters approved the arrangement, and Zilker Park was created with the bonus of a new city drinking-water supply from the springs. Zilker donated two more adjoining tracts before his death in 1934 to complete the city's 351-acre signature park. Zilker's gift was the first of many water-protection measures that would follow. He put it in more spiritual terms: "Barton Springs is a sacred place. One would be wise to listen to the springs when deciding how to care for this land and these waters in the future. . . . It would be a wrongful thing for this beauty spot to be owned by any individual, and it ought to belong to all the people of Austin."

Barton Springs was changed in 1929 from a series of swimming holes between cliffs and hillsides to a three-acre dammed pool with a mostly natural rock bottom and sidewalks surrounding much of it. A wooden bathhouse survived major floods that repeatedly closed the pool in 1935 and 1936, but it was razed in 1946 and replaced with the stone and concrete structure that's still in place today. Floods continue to interrupt swimming, but a bypass tunnel built under the north sidewalk in 1976 diverts much of the muddy, debris-filled creek waters after heavy rains. The tunnel and the upstream dam's five-foot height is no match, however, for the severe floods that can hurtle down Barton Creek through the greenbelt's canyons. The pool was closed for weeks after major flooding in 1981 and 2002.

The popularity of the pool grew substantially in the 1960s and 1970s as Austin moved beyond its small-town status as primarily a university and state government center. Despite earlier desegregation steps across the South, it wasn't until 1963 that Barton Springs was integrated after protests by local African Americans. In 1978, more than 421,000 people were admitted to the pool when the city's population was just 332,000. Today, with an Austin metropolitan population of two million, more than 800,000 people a year pay to swim at the historic pool.

Changes to the pool's aging bathhouse and nearby areas may be coming. A new group called the Barton Springs Conservancy is working with the city on a rehabilitation plan for the bathhouse. The conservancy also has proposed building a Visitor Education Center in the park to better engage people in the environmental splendors of the springs and the aquifer. Without a comprehensive parking and shuttles plan, summertime traffic jams near the pool will continue.

All of which brings me again to the main entrance of Barton Springs, greeted by a bronze statue of three men, two in bathing suits and one with his pants rolled up. They are conversing on a rock ledge, one holding a book. The 1994 sculpture of Austin writers J. Frank Dobie and Walter Prescott Webb and naturalist Roy Bedichek depicts their frequent gatherings at Barton Springs Pool in the 1950s.

In 1926, Barton Springs Pool featured a wooden bathhouse but still resembled a creek. (Source: C01824BS, Austin History Center, Austin Public Library)

Nearby are four information panels that sum up the serious aspects of this place to swim, frolic, and sunbathe. "Geology and Hydrology" explains how the Edwards Aquifer works as a water supply and source of the springs. "Home of the Salamanders" tells about the rare aquatic creatures living in the springs. "Stewardship" is a call to conserve water and protect the area's watersheds from pollution. "Human History" is the brief story of early settlers, Zilker Park's origins, and longtime parks director Beverly Sheffield.

A more youth-friendly free "Splash" exhibit in the bathhouse building approximates what a trip into the Edwards Aquifer might be like. Faux tunnels and caves wind past interactive displays focused on the Austin-area creeks that both replenish the aquifer and are fed by it. I go through the line to pay my three-dollar (now five) pool entry fee, then once again absorb the breathtaking view from atop the hillside.

The pool is enormous—997 feet long and 145 feet at its widest point on the downstream end. It is not a perfect rectangle, narrowing in the middle and irreg-

Early-morning swimmers can find space for laps at Barton Springs Pool.

ular where natural cliffs define the south side toward the upstream dam. The colors of the unchlorinated water range from the dark greens of deeper sections to pale blue in the shallows where a white limestone bottom reflects the sky. Trees—stately pecans, oaks, and cottonwoods—provide shade on the two hillsides along the pool. In recent years, a wider variety of saplings have been planted to ensure a healthier arboriculture. It is, indeed, a place to absorb nature despite concrete walls and sidewalks along most of the perimeter, a few stairs and railings into the water, nine lifeguard stands, and a single diving board.

Somehow, even when summer afternoon crowds swell, it all feels like a secret swimming hole with chilly fresh spring water and an uneven bottom of gravel, rock ledges, and cement slabs. Years ago, I occasionally would join a handful of early-morning swimmers making slow laps of the entire length of the pool enshrouded in the mists of air and water temperatures colliding. That quietude was what drew a fearless friend of mine and her three girlfriends there on a recent February morning for a predawn swim—without the encumbrances of swimsuits. They were discreet in the near darkness, slipping off their clothing at poolside just before starting their mile-long series of laps. A couple of other swimmers already in the water paid no attention. "Serene" and "mermaid-like" was how the naked swimmers later described the just-for-fun experience. While the pool is not clothing optional, it has long been a place where a few women swim and sunbathe topless. When hippies in the 1970s discovered there was no city ordinance against going without a top at Barton Springs, the practice caught on. It has all but sputtered out now. The occasional sunbather minus the top of a two-piece elicits only ho-hums or a few kiddie snickers.

What is au naturel for every swimmer once immersed in the water is the appearance and feel of the pool itself. The bottom is a patchwork of waving, leaf-shaped sagittaria grass growing from the silt and gravel. Slippery algae hug other areas. Minnow-sized Mexican tetras, large sunfish, and some bass and catfish swim freely in the pool. So do a few turtles and lots of crayfish. Hardly ever does a swimmer spot one of the tiny rare salamanders that live under small rocks and in limestone crevasses near where the spring water gushes up.

The greatest wonder for me is Main Spring at the bottom of the pool's middle section. The strongest spring outlets emerge about seventeen feet down, not far upstream from the diving board. The water that flows out has averaged 32 million gallons a day since record keeping began in 1894, but extreme conditions of droughts and floods have put the flow as low as 6 million gallons a day and as high as 166 million gallons a day.

The pool's water temperature averages sixty-eight to seventy degrees, a bit warmer than that in shallow parts in the summer and a little colder in the winter in deep spots. It's always fun to watch visitors react to what is not the usual temperature of a Texas swimming pool. They enter gingerly, shiver for a while, and talk nonstop about how chilly the water is, though nothing is more refreshing to me than a dip on a hundred-degree day.

Because Barton Springs is a habitat for two endangered species of aquatic salamanders, the pool is not scrubbed free of all algae. In the 1970s, the pool was lowered substantially for cleanings and hoses as big as those on fire trucks were used to blast away the algae. Now that the salamanders are protected, small air hoses and gentle buffers are used in the shallow areas and on steps on Thursdays from 9:00 a.m. to 7:00 p.m. when the pool is closed for cleaning. The water level is lowered only a few times a year for major cleanings. Big hoses are still necessary in the deep end of the pool where silt and gravel collect, but conditions have improved since the removal in 2011 of tons of such debris after major flooding.

There's never just one "scene" at Barton Springs on a crowded day. Out-of-state and foreign tourists are heard. So are local musicians who pick guitars or tap out drumbeats. Sunbathers on rafts in the deep end and on the grass covering the hillsides hardly move. Klatches of seniors who have been coming to the pool for decades gather under a propped-up old pecan tree along the north sidewalk. Toddlers learn to swim in the shallow end as parents hover nearby. And count on seeing at least one determined lap swimmer with a snorkel cutting through the multitudes in the water.

Barton Springs is a people's pool and a sanctuary for living animals and plants. Austin filmmaker Karen Kocher aptly chose the title *Living Springs* for an internet and television documentary series she began in 2016. The continuing project by the University of Texas senior lecturer highlights the life cycle of water as it moves from rainfall to the aquifer to the springs. It also, of course, shows the salamanders that hide out in the pool and are its most well-known residents.

As my story of Barton Creek began to take shape, I was especially eager to see up close the Barton Springs salamander and Austin blind salamander. How deep these creatures would take me was a surprise. I would watch meticulous counts and identifying photography at all four spring sites in and around the pool. I followed a city biologist intent on finding the salamanders farther upstream on Barton Creek and on Onion Creek. I discovered a seldom-seen breeding facility that ensures a population of the salamanders will live on should a calamitous event occur.

Long walks along parts of Barton Creek that I never knew existed and repeated dips in the pool reaffirmed for me why Barton Springs is dubbed the soul of the city. The joy on the faces of people in or around the water reflects that soul. I'll see it again and again visiting many citizens, Barton Creek dwellers, conservation landowners, and environmentalists who joyfully protect what we love.

2 SAVING SALAMANDERS

Searching For, Counting, and Raising Two Endangered Species

Biologist Tom Devitt makes a casual prediction as we climb into a city truck to search for endangered salamanders upstream on Barton Creek and a couple of its many tributaries: "Just so you know, it's very unlikely we'll find any salamanders today." My hopes of discovering a salamander living far from Barton Springs Pool cannot be dashed that easily. Tom and his young associate Brad Nissen established a track record in 2017 of finding the endangered Barton Springs salamanders at sites as distant as Onion Creek. That creek and its watershed south of US 290 recharge the underground Edwards Aquifer at three times the volume of Barton Creek. But no known populations of the Barton Springs and Austin blind salamanders approach the numbers found in and around Austin's most famous springs-fed pool. What Tom and Brad want to learn is if there are any unique differences in those species found elsewhere.

The two scientists work for the City of Austin's Watershed Protection Department. On this day, they plan to check spring sites where they previously stashed, of all things, mop heads. Instead of mopping floors, the clumps of white cotton strings are used as artificial habitats for the salamanders. The critters like to hide amid the tangles stuffed into spring outlets. The mop heads also make dinner-table settings because tiny bugs that the salamanders eat are attracted to the strings, too.

Our first stop on this search-and-capture adventure is the Barton Creek Habitat Preserve's Sweetwater tract on the west side of Texas 71 near the town of Bee Cave. Tom unlocks the gate with a code provided by The Nature Conservancy, which manages the preserve's forty-one hundred acres on both sides of the highway with four miles of Barton Creek. A half mile in, the old ranch road is too rough to drive farther. Checking his cell phone's Google Earth pin for the unnamed spring, Tom says it will be a bit of a hike through dense woods. Call that an understatement as we duck under masses of cedar branches, some from old-growth trees with gnarly trunks nearly two-feet wide. We dodge or carefully pull aside greenbrier vines. (Birds like to eat the plant's berries, and the thorns like to eat shirts and pants.) The aim is to claw our way down to a small Barton Creek tributary stream.

When we finally reach the water, I'm pleased that Tom and Brad recognize the narrow stream that is barely moving and less than a foot deep in most

City biologists search through mop heads placed to attract salamanders.

places. We pick our way atop the banks and sometimes in the creek bed to three separate spring sites where mop heads were inserted a few weeks earlier. It's the same story at each stop: The biologists crouch down to the discharge points in limestone cracks and mossy overhangs. They remove the mop heads and carefully pick through the strings with a net underneath. No salamanders. They reinsert the mop heads and we move on.

Tom is encouraged because he does find tiny arthropods, bugs that live in the aquifer and sometimes come to the surface in springs. Just as the salamanders do. He puts several of the creatures in a canister of alcohol so they can be positively identified in a laboratory. We hike back up through the thickets and drive to the next stop at the Shield Ranch. This is the biggest conservation easement property on Barton Creek, a spread of sixty-eight hundred acres with hills and valleys and six miles of Barton Creek. Tom's destination on the ranch is a tributary called Holman Hollow. The stream looks like the one on the Sweetwater tract, but access is easier just off a gravel road. But, again, no salamanders. And this time no invertebrate bugs either. Tom decides to pull the mop heads that have been in the springs for three months. "I won't come back here for a while, if ever," he says. Yet as we head to the truck, he spots a crayfish in the water eating a bunch of frog eggs. "Wow, now that's interesting," the biologist pronounces. Maybe there is more life in this stream to explore later.

We head back toward Austin to Travis Country, a subdivision built in the 1970s above the south side of what is now the Barton Creek Wilderness Park. Numerous trails lead down to the creek through sun-baked dry uplands pocked with prickly pear cactus. When we arrive at the creek, it is, comparatively, a jungle with towering shade trees and spring greenery everywhere. Turning onto a well-worn path along the creek, we come to our final search site. I probably would have walked right past the two small springs flowing from a cliff face.

Tom and Brad pull the mop heads from each spring and sift through the strings. With no luck, they start turning over small rocks in an inches-deep stream running from the springs down into Barton Creek. Just a few minutes into their search: "I got one," yells Brad.

"You're shittin' me," Tom yells back as he scrambles toward Brad with his net. He puts the net in the water just downstream of where Brad crouches.

"I saw it for sure. The tail was wiggling out from under a rock. It was right in my fingers but slipped out," Brad confesses.

Tom carefully searches the net, now filled with leaves and sediment. "It's here! We got it," he shouts. High fives all around before Tom displays to photographer Alberto Martinez the nearly two-inch pinkish-brown salamander. Then he puts it in a Hydro flask of water from the spring. "This is unbelievable," he says. "Brad is good luck for us. I never thought we'd

A rare discovery made on Barton Creek far upstream from Barton Springs.

actually get one here. You've witnessed a new local site for the Barton Springs salamander, one of the world's rarest species. Finding one here on the greenbelt, right where people hike by, is awesome."

The biologists continue looking under rock after rock in the stream, but they find nothing more. After half an hour, we return to the truck with the single salamander. What will happen back at the office? I ask. "Unfortunately, this guy will become a specimen," Tom says. "We'll preserve him in alcohol for laboratory work." DNA tissue samples will tell if there are any differences in this salamander and the ones in the springs near the mouth of Barton Creek. A DNA sequencing study began in 2016 with the University of Texas trying to determine the genetic diversity within the species. It could result in a better estimate of the total population and more understanding of the connection between water quality in the creeks and that in the aquifer. Tom also will photograph the specimen found on the greenbelt and report the new locality to the US Fish and Wildlife Service, which oversees recovery plans for endangered species.

The total count at all the remote spring sites sampled by the end of 2017 was twenty individuals—all Barton Springs salamanders, no Austin blind salamanders. One of those was found on another trip to the greenbelt spring site. They've also been found at a spring on Lady Bird Lake upriver from Barton Creek and in a well in Manchaca. Others have been found in Onion Creek at Camp Ben McCulloch and on private ranches on that creek. (Those discoveries in Hays County have been cited by residents fighting the City of Dripping Springs' application for a state permit to release treated sewage effluent into a tributary of Onion Creek.)

Tom, who also leads quarterly salamander counts in Barton Springs Pool, will keep searching the outlying sites. The greater value than any one specimen's life, he says, is to learn more about the life cycle of these entirely aquatic amphibians. Understanding where and how they move around the aquifer and

Protected Central Texas Salamanders

Barton Springs salamander (*Eurycea sosorum*)
Listed under the federal Endangered Species Act in 1997, the salamander was named to reference the Save Our Springs (SOS) citizens' campaign and city land-use ordinance approved by voters in 1992. The salamander depends on the flow and quality of water from the springs of the Edwards Aquifer. It is found primarily in springs in and around Barton Springs Pool and only in Travis and Hays Counties under rocks, in gravel, or among aquatic vascular plants and algae. It feeds primarily on arthropods, a classification of bugs with external skeletons and segmented bodies. Growing to about two and a half inches in length, the salamander has external gills and skin color of brown mottling over blue-gray to yellowish tones.

Austin blind salamander (*Eurycea waterlooensis*)
Listed under the Endangered Species Act in 2013, the salamander name refers to Waterloo, the first name for Austin. The salamander has no image-forming lenses but displays subdermal eye spots behind its flattened nose. It is mostly restricted to subterranean cavities of the Edwards Aquifer and is found only in Travis County in and around Barton Springs Pool. The salamander feeds on water bugs, plant material, and arthropods. It grows to about three inches in length and has pearly-white to translucent lavender skin color, with red external gills.

Related separate species dependent on Edwards Aquifer
The San Marcos salamander (threatened species) is found at the headwaters of the San Marcos River. The Texas blind salamander (endangered species) is found in water-filled caverns along the San Marcos River. The Jollyville Plateau salamander (threatened species) is found in the springs and caves north of the Colorado River in Travis and Williamson Counties.

Barton Springs salamander. (Photo by Tom Devitt)

Austin blind salamander. (Photo by Tom Devitt)

springs will help ensure the species' future, says the biologist, and serve to protect water and land for humans as well. The salamanders are like the proverbial canary in a coal mine. If they are present in healthy numbers, it shows the water quality is good. If they are declining, all the thousands of people who swim In Barton Springs should be worried.

Another Austin front for salamander research and conservation is managed by Dee Ann Chamberlain, the virtual mother to hundreds of the creatures at a little-known captive-breeding facility. She watches over a population of 350 Barton Springs salamanders and 50 Austin blind salamanders that live in one big room stacked floor to ceiling with aquariums about the size of an average home fish tank. Why keep them in tanks when they are accessible to scientists at the four Barton Springs sites? "The main reason is to have a population that could be released in the wild to reproduce. Our master plan under the Endangered Species Act is to be able to do that if a disaster occurred. A major spill of toxic chemicals could take years and years to clean up," she tells me on a visit to her plain concrete-block building with a colorful salamander mosaic on one side.

It's obvious Dee Ann has become attached to her charges over the years since she started the captive-breeding program in 1998 as part of the city's conservation plan to protect the endangered species. The building on the grounds of the Austin Nature & Science Center that now houses the salamanders was built in 2008. It is not open to the public. "We talk about our salamanders as individuals," she says. "We identify each one, photograph it, and give it a number in our database."

The oldest and biggest of all the individuals Dee Ann cares for is an Austin blind salamander, which she found as a small juvenile in November 1998 at Sunken Garden. Now grown to about 3.5 inches long, the pale, eyeless salamander is nearly twenty years old. It is rivaled in age at the facility by two Barton Springs salamanders a couple of years younger. No one knows what age any of the lungless, externally gilled salamanders might reach in captivity. Some species of larger land-based salamanders can live for forty years or more. "It's a pretty interesting animal," Dee Ann says of the two species. Her smile reveals how much this soft-spoken biologist loves her job. "Salamanders in general are cool. They are so diverse, with some on land and some in water and some that move from one environment to another."

In 2001, Dee Ann wrote a scientific paper along with University of Texas biologists David Hillis, Thomas Wilcox, and Paul Chippindale titled "A New Species of Subterranean Blind Salamander . . . from Austin, Texas, and a Systematic Revision of Central Texas Paedomorphic Salamanders." (Paedomorphic is from paedomorphosis, an evolutionary process in which larval features are retained in an adult, possibly giving rise to a wholly new organism.) The paper recommended the common name of Austin blind salamander and a scientific name of *Eurycea waterlooensis*. A dozen years later—after Austin blinds were found at all four spring sites in and around Barton Springs Pool but predominantly at Sunken Garden—the federal government listed the species as endangered, in part because its aquifer habitat is so vulnerable. Far more Barton Springs salamanders are counted each quarter, but Austin blinds spend most of their lives in the subterranean recesses of the Edwards Aquifer. Why some make their way to the surface through the springs is not known.

At the captive-breeding facility, water in the tanks comes from a nearby well that pumps groundwater originating from the aquifer. Surface water would risk introducing contaminants. Dee Ann walks from one rack of tanks to another, showing off the two species and noting the coloration and size differences between adults and juveniles. The salamanders navigate at different levels in the water with slow swishes of their tails. A few of the critters cling with their limbs to strands of wispy white fabric floating in the tanks

Salamanders dwell in tanks at the city's captive-breeding facility.

like rest stops. Dee Ann easily nets a few salamanders to display for the photographer. Several minutes out of the water do not seem to bother them, but they could not survive for an hour that way.

Clusters of pale eggs about the size of a pinhead are attached to the fabric in a few of the tanks. Egg laying is unpredictable and unwanted. Dee Ann says some breeding females have deposited an average of fifteen eggs every month, but the facility cannot hold an unchecked number of salamanders. "We need to manage each population in captivity for genetic diversity. Therefore, we have culled eggs, at times, when we had reproduction before we had a chance to separate the males from the females," Dee Ann explains. It's a balancing act to keep a stable population. The usual mortality rate is about 10 percent. "We rarely collect from the wild, and, currently, about ninety percent of our salamanders are captive-raised," she says.

I tell her about my boyhood joy of finding a few red salamanders (*Pseudotriton ruber*) during a camping trip to Smoky Mountains National Park. The common, mostly terrestrial salamanders came home with me, a likely illicit move even in the early 1960s. I tended to them in a nice terrarium with a water dish. But a year later the population had multiplied to far too many to suit my mother, so I let them go in a nearby patch of woods. Dee Ann seems amused—and interested—in my story. She says she would like to know more about the lives in the wild of the two species she cares for and studies day after day.

"We don't know a lot about their habits in terms of exactly where they are found in the aquifer, where they are going, and how they reproduce there and what they eat there. How would we access that? Maybe a camera could be developed, like ones that have been used in water wells, to show us what is going on inside the aquifer. It's probably not impossible, although the logistics would be difficult," she says. "We don't know how deep they go and how they deal with the pressures there," she continues. "How long do they spend at the surface in the springs? We don't even know what percent of them we are seeing there."

She notes that the endangered species permit plan for her facility "is to deal only with the salamanders at the springs in and near the pool, not upstream sites. Eventually we'll probably look at ones upstream." My visit with Dee Ann ends with her voicing the lament of many dedicated scientists: "The more we learn, the more questions we have."

To understand the Barton Springs habitats where the salamanders are found, counted, photographed, and returned to the wild, I take a walking tour with city biologist Donelle Robinson. Discovery of the first salamander in the springs was reported in 1946. It wasn't confirmed as a distinct species of aquatic salamander until decades later. We meet at the main entrance of Barton Springs Pool and walk to a nearby active construction site above the pool. Black tarps shield what is going on inside. We slip through flaps to get to the gate of Eliza Spring.

The local Elks Club built the oval-shaped, rock-and-concrete amphitheater around several natural spring outlets in 1903. Four terraces gave club members and guests a place to enjoy the sun. They could wade or sit in water flowing through holes drilled in a concrete slab at the bottom of the amphitheater. Today, Eliza Spring is locked up to protect the salamanders there. Donelle has the key and we step down to just above the fifteen-foot-wide bottom of the amphitheater. The water is only about a foot deep on this day, but it rises as rains produce greater flows from the springs.

Nathan Bendik, another salamander biologist, is sitting on a terrace, busy with research work on his laptop computer. I ask him why he thinks the Elks built this structure apart from the main swimming area of the creek. The idea, Nathan surmises, was that "they wanted to create their own air-conditioning hole." The steep, walled interior of the amphithe-

An expanded salamander habitat was constructed at Eliza Spring in 2017.

ater was cooler than the sun-drenched main springs before the pool was built. In recent years, city biologists have maintained a single layer of fist-sized rocks on the concrete floor of Eliza Spring. The salamanders live under those rocks, feeding on arthropods in the water. They rarely swim to the surface. Their external crimson gills work best when the springs flow at a steady, moderate rate, Donelle says.

The salamanders don't do well in droughts. Recent counts at Eliza and the other nearby springs have been low compared to the numbers before the 2008 and 2009 droughts. Eliza's flow then was diminished but never ceased entirely. Still, counts at Eliza have yielded higher numbers than in Barton Springs Pool. Nathan thinks that is "because of the environment. They're not disturbed by swimmers and it's not deep water. It's hard to say why for sure. All we can do is speculate."

The construction project at Eliza in 2017 replaced the amphitheater's old, partially collapsed buried drainage pipe with a "daylighting" channel. Now the spring water flows down the channel and into the pool's creek-bypass tunnel. A barrier keeps the salamanders from going into the tunnel but allows the water to pass through. The primary goal is "to increase the habitat space, which should increase the population of the salamanders here," Donelle tells me. Today an open-air, seventy-foot-long landscaped stream sits behind fencing that allows pool-goers a glimpse of the new habitat. "Our hope is that the salamanders will navigate into the Eliza stream, where we have another layer of rocks for them to live under. It is part of our long-term recovery plan for the species," says Donelle.

Shade trees were planted to help keep the channel cool. Leaves that fall in the water give invertebrate bugs something to munch on. Then the salamanders, in turn, have more invertebrates to dine on. In future years, the concrete floor of Eliza Spring will be removed to give the salamanders a more natural environment. "But that will be its own project," says Donelle. "We don't want to disturb them too much at once. It will be better to wait until the stream has been well established and colonized."

Moving along on our tour, we cross over Barton Creek to another spring in a wooded area downstream of the pool. This spring has been called Sunken Garden since Depression-era terrace work. Larger than Eliza Spring, Sunken Garden drains into the creek via a culvert and stream through the woods. Two rock terraces wide enough for picnicking in years past encircle the walled-in springs. Water bubbles up in a dark, shallow pool below the terraces. Donelle unlocks the gate and we walk down to the springs. Here several string mop heads float in the water. The salamanders that don't favor hiding under rocks on the bottom apparently like the strings. I can't think of a more economical and low-tech solution to keeping the salamanders happy and making searches for them easier.

A lot of sand sediment covers the bottom of Sunken Garden. Donelle says an estimated eight tons of sand comes up each year in the spring discharge water. Some of it is removed periodically. A couple of months after the tour with Donelle, I meet her at Sunken Garden for a salamander count. The results are disappointing. She found only one small juvenile salamander in the murky water. She says the site has not had much of a population since the droughts of several years ago when the water flow up through the sediment was minimal and the stream down to the creek dried up entirely.

Sunken Garden is where the Austin blind salamander was first found in 1998. "No one realized that the Austin blind was its own species to look for before that," says Donelle. It took another fifteen years of studies and finds to identify it as a distinct species and to win protected status as endangered. The highest Austin blind counts at each spring were forty-four in 2002 at Sunken Garden, twelve at Eliza Spring in 2006, five at the pool's Main Spring in 2010, and one in 2013 at Upper Spring in Barton Creek.

Before leaving Sunken Garden, I look for any sign of who built the terracing. It's on a small bronze plaque below the main entrance steps. It reads "1937–38 National Youth Administration." The New Deal jobs program put needy youth to work on such public projects, much like the larger Civilian Conservation Corps for adults. In Texas, the NYA was headed up by Lyndon B. Johnson from 1935 until 1937, when he was elected to Congress.

The project was designed as a gathering and picnicking place. A flagstone stage and picnic tables to seat three hundred were built on the stone terraces. From the opening of Sunken Garden and into the 1990s, the public could freely come and go onto the terraces and wade into the spring. Then the city fenced and gated the site to protect the salamanders that likely had been visiting there for decades, too. A city plan has been proposed that would rebuild the crumbling stonework at Sunken Garden and improve the channel of water leaving the spring. No funding or date for that project is set.

Next, Donelle and I follow a trail upstream along the creek and past the south entrance to Barton Springs Pool. Apartments perch on the bluffs above where the creek is heavily wooded on both sides. An informational sign with color photographs of the salamanders sticks up among the trees and rocks near the Upper Spring site. The spring cannot be fenced because of its location in the creek, so it risks being vandalized or endangered by careless waders disturbing the rocks at the base of the flow. "This is the most natural of our springs because there hasn't been any construction around the outlet here," says Donelle. I look for the spring but see nothing as water rushes by on each side of a narrow strip of trees and rocks. Donelle points to a spot close to the shoreline with just a foot or two of water. The spring is a gurgling bubble of clear water about the size and shape of a football above the creek surface. "The flow rate here is much less than in the pool and other sites," she says.

In May 2017, when the stream flow was about average, one adult Barton Springs salamander was found in the creek twenty feet from the spring outlet. The site dried up entirely in the 2008–9 drought across Central Texas. But in the wet spring of 2010, a surprising 99 salamanders were counted in Upper Spring. None of the other spring locations have fully recovered from the drought. At Eliza, 1,210 salamanders were found in a count just before the drought set in and 529 in April 2013. At Sunken Garden, 123 were found before the drought and just 8 following it. At the pool's Main Spring, the count was 439 before the drought. The highest number since was 135 in November 2015. It is not known how many salamanders inhabiting the springs were able to safely move into the aquifer or if they died when the water volume decreased.

Donelle's final stop on our tour is where the water for Barton Springs Pool is produced from sites in the middle of the pool called Main Spring. Every minute of the day and night, cool, clean water from the aquifer surges out from crevasses and ledges at the bottom of the pool. In very wet years, up to eighty-five million gallons of water a day comes up. In very dry years, the volume drops to under ten million gallons a day. This spring has never gone dry in recorded history. The deepest of three groupings of outlets is seventeen feet below the surface, just a few yards from the pool's single diving board. The other side outlets are in ledges that form a V shape around the deeper one. I first felt the power of this spring's flow in the late 1970s when I brought my children to the pool on cleaning day to swim. We would dive down to try to touch where the water rushed out. At that time, we had no idea we could be disturbing salamanders living there.

Weeks after Donelle's tour, biologists come to the closed pool on cleaning day for a quarterly salamander count. Nathan Bendik is first in the water with his scuba gear. He surfaces after just a couple of minutes

Divers bring up netted salamanders for regular counts at Barton Springs Pool.

and utters a few choice curse words. "Someone has moved the rocks—even a small boulder! This habitat has been disturbed," he shouts to his fellow scientists. A pool manager is summoned, and they discuss how lifeguards are supposed to stop anyone who appears to be diving to the bottom where the springs flow from cracks and under rocks and ledges. It's tough to spot swimmers doing that when the pool is crowded with bodies. The manager says perhaps another sign is needed at the side of the pool telling people not to disturb the bottom or move rocks. One sign already notes the endangered salamanders live under the rocks.

Nathan resumes his dive, staying down with two other biologists for nearly an hour. When the divers surface, he is all smiles and gives a thumbs-up when I ask if many salamanders were captured. They are brought to the surface in nets for each one to be quickly photographed and then released back into the springs. Skin colorations and patterns vary with individuals so they can be identified and tracked if caught again.

"We just started working out over the past year how best to catch them and bring them up for photographs," says Nathan. The divers submerge with two-foot-long, fine-meshed net tubes. Each tube has a closed end and a drawstring end. When divers turn over small rocks on the pool bottom and spot salamanders underneath, they are nudged into a tube. It's not an easy task given the amphibians' ability to quickly swim away with flicks of their tails. Once the nets are filled with several salamanders each, they are placed in a large wire cage brought to the bottom. That way the divers do not have to surface until the cage is filled with netted collections. Misses are frequent during the underwater chases. Nathan describes one to fellow diver Brad Nissen: "I just missed this big, beautiful salamander. It was really opaque and pretty. I just sat down there staring at my empty net for a few minutes."

Also counting salamanders is team leader Tom Devitt and Dee Ann Chamberlain, manager of the captive-breeding program across the road. Tom says the counting process is not a perfect survey because the salamanders are difficult to spot and capture amid the strong spring flows in the pool. When Dee Ann surfaces for a new tank of air, she tells me: "It's tough down there. That took a lot of energy. I just found one small one, but I'm going back down." Nathan advises her to concentrate on the areas with small rocks, not where there is a lot of sand and silt on the bottom.

After a cage filled with net tubes is brought to the side of the pool, several young lifeguards stop cleaning duty to gather around the divers. Most have never seen a salamander up close. The catch is brought to a camera stand on the pool deck, where the divers put each salamander in a plastic tray of water. The amphibians are photographed one by one and recorded on a log sheet. "Because every salamander has a unique pigment pattern on the head and back, we can keep track of each salamander year after year. It's just like a fingerprint identification," Donelle tells me.

The total count that day after two dive sessions by four biologists: twenty. That includes one quarter-inch juvenile salamander that appears weak and can barely swing its tail to swim. Dee Ann says she'll keep that one to take back to her breeding facility. Brad suggests that perhaps they should not be netting juveniles under an inch long because they could be hurt in the process. "It must be traumatic for them, and they're just weaker," he says.

One of the pool salamanders photographed has a couple of eggs attached to its body (gravid is the scientific term). Biologists are not sure where most eggs are deposited and hatched. Deep in the aquifer or in the springs? Only a few eggs have been found during the quarterly counts. The count ends, like many others, with more questions than answers. The salamander biologists know they still have much to learn about the endangered species that keep Barton Springs such a protected, life-filled place.

3 FAMILY LANDS

The Starks' Summer Camp and the Family Legacy of Truman Breed

Richard Stark grew up walking down the middle of Barton Creek and exploring its banks around his family's Sports Country Camp northwest of Dripping Springs. In the summer of 1992, he decided to hike the creek all the way to Austin. Forty rugged miles of discovery awaited. He was friendly with neighbors near the camp on Bell Springs Road. Most were ranchers who, when he was a young boy, had no problem with him climbing through their fences and keeping an eye out for any trouble with their livestock. Richard had visited the "killer Bell Spring" on a downstream property that pumps through a rock face. But he didn't know exactly where the creek would lead him beyond that or what he would find on the mostly private lands he would cross. Richard invited his friends Andy Hollon, Travis Crow, and Mark Van Dyne, fellow college students then, to skirt and slosh the length of the creek with him. At the time, they had been reading the books of Tom Brown Jr., a best-selling naturalist and tracker from the Northeast.

"We loved Barton Creek and wanted to experience all of it, practice our nature-awareness skills, and have an adventure," Richard recalls. They would take their time on the trek, camping two nights. They had heard—correctly—it was legal given Texas' waterway laws establishing public access in the creek bed itself. That's why kayakers and canoers can be found on many stretches of Barton Creek when it's flowing enough to be fun and they can put in at a public road crossing or the Austin greenbelt.

As the sun came up on an August morning, the four buddies started out where Barton Creek passes under a small bridge on Ranch Road 12. Richard's father drove them over to that spot because the first leg of their trip would be through the large cattle and goat ranch of Henry and Kay Brooks, longtime friends of Travis's family. Andy remembers the start: "It was brutally hot, and the bull nettles and fire ants combined to leave our legs in pretty rough shape since we all wore shorts. We'd make periodic stops in the deeper holes along the creek to cool ourselves off and discuss whether we had lost our minds to even attempt such an adventure. Being the age we were, our discussions often wandered from the actual hike into the familiar topics of pretty

As a youth on Barton Creek, Richard Stark Jr. found enough artifacts to fill a room.

girls and cold beer. I don't recall ever looking over maps ahead of that trip, so I never had a good sense of where we were at any given time—aside from occasional landmarks that Richard would point out."

From the Brookses' ranch, the hikers followed the wildly winding creek as it dips south along what was then the sprawling Hazy Hills Ranch, owned by the oil-rich Townes-Peyton family out of Houston. In 2017, a developer began building one thousand houses on the ranchland now called Headwaters. Turning back toward the northeast, the hikers arrived at the Trautwein Road crossing and a large, well-known swimming hole. Time to cool down and chill out a while. When they resumed their trek, a friendly, short-legged small dog started followed them and they couldn't shoo him away. "We dubbed him Nettles, and he kept up with us for the rest of the trip," Richard says.

Onward toward Fitzhugh Road and past Willie Nelson's old ranch compound. The singer had found peace and quiet with his family there in the early 1970s, but after his *Red Headed Stranger* album took off, "there were people showing up at the ranch who thought I could lay hands on them and heal their crippled limbs," Nelson says in his autobiography. "We built a six-foot-high wall with stones three feet thick. . . . We strung electrified wire across the top of the wall and stuck up signs that said No Trespassing, No Admittance, No Hunting, No Kidding." It didn't work. Nelson moved on, trading floats in Barton Creek for mountain views in Colorado long before Richard's trek through the property. After the Fitzhugh crossing, the hikers soon were on a far corner of the much larger Shield Ranch. Here they found a secluded spot beside the creek to camp the first night. The looping stream snakes for six miles across the picture-postcard ranch, which in 1998 would become water-protection conservation land.

Travis recalls other parts of the creek where dense patches of nettles and plentiful seed ticks were like plagues: "After the first few miles the nettles had numbed my legs so much that pain was no longer felt. We hiked along the creek, in the creek, and tried to anticipate shortcuts to cut cross-country. In my great wisdom of twenty-one, I brought an old army backpack loaded with canned goods and water. It weighed about eighty pounds and about killed me." There were many good moments, however. Travis says that water holes "emerged around bends of the creek like we were old settlers or Indians seeing this country and its beauty for the first time." Deer, armadillos, and opossums scattered from the creek banks as they approached, and small fish raced ahead when they splashed through the rippling water. What none of the hikers had expected in a thick stand of cedars was to come face-to-face with a full-grown, two thousand–pound bison. Just ten yards from them, the enormous animal stood still and stared. Then they noticed its red halter. The bison was a pet they had seen before on Don Chapman's property, which they apparently were crossing. Neither the men nor the bison made any sudden movements, and the four weary ones slowly moved on downstream.

Below the then-quiet village of Bee Cave they passed the old creekside house where famed Texas writer J. Frank Dobie spent his last days in the 1960s before the house became a University of Texas writers' retreat. Then they saw the log cabin remnants from mid-1800s settlers at the confluence of the creek with Little Barton Creek near the Texas 71 highway. Climbing over an old low-water concrete crossing, the friends looked up at the towering highway bridge above them. It was getting dark, and they had figured this would be a good place to make camp for their second night. "But first we called my dad from the Bohls family place just downstream of 71 to say we were OK. This was pre-cell days. We knew the Bohls and had arranged with them to restock our water supply there," Richard remembers. The hikers probably could have survived drinking the creek water, but they wisely packed enough water in bottles and canteens for each day's journey.

The next morning, they moved on through Bee

Cave. They stomped through the four miles of Barton Creek where developers had already installed fire hydrants and staked out roads for houses. The land would be saved by The Nature Conservancy in 1994 as a preserve for endangered bird species. Roughly parallel to Bee Caves Road at this point, the creek passed behind and in front of new and old neighborhoods. They were bound to stir up unfriendly dogs and serious trouble. Richard remembers: "We did have a couple of interesting encounters with locals. One time we got warning shots up in the trees but weren't sure from where. Another time we were escorted away from the creek to the front of the property. That guy wanted to know where we were from, and we told him Dripping Springs. He said, 'Well you should know what climbing on a fence does to a man.'"

They found another place to pick up the creek and head downstream after the pointed reminder about property rights. "It was something we kind of expected," Richard adds. At the Barton Creek Country Club, where the creek curves around a golf course, the hikers encountered strange looks but also water spigots and a restroom. They were happy for the respite in not-so-wild surroundings.

It was late and near closing time for Barton Creek Square Mall when they arrived at Loop 360. They still had another five miles or so on the city greenbelt and the creek's most rock-strewn sections before they'd reach Barton Springs Pool and the cafés nearby on Barton Springs Road. "When we got to the mall, we were done," Richard says. "We called Dad from Sears for a ride back home." Travis remembers, sitting under oaks on the west side of the mall and waiting: "I know that we all looked like hell because everyone that passed stared at us in disbelief." On the way back home, the friends returned Nettles to where they had found him. It was an exhausting but fun trek. They celebrated with beers and a buttermilk pie Susan had made for them.

Three years later, Richard and Andy decided to try the hike upstream from Austin to Dripping Springs.

They picked an April night when the full moon would be out and left from their duplex on Enfield Road after work. The plan was to walk through the night and the next day with no camping. Andy remembers: "We had topo maps for this trip, and we'd spent a little time going over them before we started out. What we hadn't planned on was that the moon set around four a.m. and left us with a window of total darkness. And the temperature had dropped well below what we were ready for. I also recall it being quite a challenge to track our progress throughout the night as we periodically consulted the quad sheet to try to estimate our whereabouts. We tended to take an optimistic view of the progress we were making. But as Richard noted, nature is powerfully indifferent to one's optimism or wishful thinking."

Another challenge was simply knowing which stream to follow. "Every time we reached the confluence point of a significant tributary, we would have to choose which branch was the creek itself and which was the tributary. We guessed incorrectly more than once and had to cross-country hike back to the main creek once we'd realized our error." Some twenty-three hours of nonstop walking later, often utilizing ridges and hillside trails instead of the vegetation-heavy creek below, the two trekkers arrived at the Starks' house.

For years after the trips, when Richard came home to visit during summer camp sessions, the hikes added fuel to his stories around the fire pit. He told of being "in the presence of the creek's clear-water mystic" on his plunge into the wilderness. Young campers awed by his telling must have imagined another world in another time. Lean and fit in his mid-forties today, Richard says he would like to try that kind of creek journey again. "You want to come with me?" he asks me. It would be a tougher trip. Much of the land on both sides of Barton Creek downstream from the Starks now has higher and stronger new fences and very few farmers and ranchers with just a few rusted strands of barbed wire. The homeowners with fancy back porches and patios, pools, and security systems likely would not abide strangers in their stream whatever the legalities.

Upstream of where Richard grew up, the creek generally is less developed and has more family lands owned by old-timers such as Truman Breed Jr. On Breed's part of Barton Creek, its natural state is close to what it was when a previous owner of the property built a sturdy stone house near a bend in the creek in the 1850s. The walls are still standing. Richard spent much of his boyhood looking for and finding evidence of even earlier creek dwellers. He was six when his parents built a house and moved onto the twenty-two acres above Barton Creek that they had bought several years earlier for their youth camp. "Almost immediately he began to find evidence of Indian habitation along the creek," says his mother, Susan, "and from that he became an archaeologist."

Armed with college studies in archaeology and cultural anthropology, he methodically dug even more into the soil and rocky outcroppings on his family's acreage. What he found is an extensive, layered treasure of the history of human visitors to Barton Creek.

I visited the Starks in 2017 soon after Richard moved back to his parents' property from archaeology jobs in Hawaii and serving as teacher and headmaster at TMI Episcopal in San Antonio. Now he is an independent contractor, assessing commercial dig sites for potential archaeology relics that might be disturbed. Much of his work analyzing terrain and maps is done via computer for a Honolulu-based company. A shed along Barton Creek near the former camp's tennis courts serves as sleeping quarters when he isn't staying in Terlingua or other adventurous locales.

Before I met him, Richard sent me an email summing up his background: "The Barton Creek watershed that I grew up in had been my biggest schoolhouse and sanctuary. I grew up fishing up and down the creek and through these wanderings have accidentally found multiple prehistoric sites, fueling my interest in the past as it relates to the now." Susan says she is not surprised by his desire to live in "a very alternative way. He is a Thoreau-type fellow. Coming back to this place, especially down by the creek, gives him a feeling he couldn't find elsewhere."

Tall and lanky with straight hair reaching to his

From above the banks, the Starks witnessed raging floods and prolonged droughts.

FAMILY LANDS : 27

shoulders, Richard wants to show me something minutes after I introduce myself. I follow him down the hillside to the concrete tennis shed. There, beside his cot, is a long table filled with what he dug up nearby over years of searches: dozens and dozens of arrowheads, dart and spear points, and hide and bone scrapers of every size. Many of the artifacts are made of chert or shaped with chunks of chert. Formed from the growth of microcrystals of silicon dioxide, chert is hard and breaks at sharp angles. It is layered into deposits of limestone and other rock when groundwater moves through the rock in fractures and crevasses. Most of it is found in Texas farther west on the Edwards Plateau. Richard says chert was a prized and traded substance, probably brought into the Dripping Springs area by Native Americans who hunted and camped along Barton Creek over thousands of years.

The excitement of discovery remains in his voice years past his boyhood collection: "The makers and users of these points and tools were here, I think, in small groups and visited seasonally. There was enough erosion after that that their middens were covered over by layers of soil and rocks. My father uncovered them when he dug trenches to fight oak wilt and used a bulldozer to flatten areas down by the creek."

Richard walks across a shallow part of the creek, split by a small island of soil, stones, and young trees, to show me one midden. He picks up fist-sized, blackened rocks that he says Indians used as liners for steaming ovens built into depressions in the ground. The rocks were discarded in the trash heaps over time. Among the refuse are shells of small snails that he says could date back to when they were steamed as food snacks along with hunted game. As he explains how these long-ago cooks used their ovens, two Cooper's hawks screech overhead because we're close to their nest.

I ask him how he can find so many Indian points, chert, and oven rocks amid the scramble of brush, riverbed stones, and crumbling limestone ledges along the sides of the creek. "You have to have an eye for it and I'm really into it. I know where to look after there's been erosion or where an armadillo has been digging. I picked up sixteen arrowheads in one place here after a rain. It was a quiver full. Another time I dug a hole to bury a dog of mine and discovered the ribs of a bison."

His mother says she remembers that from an early age Richard had "this amazing sensitivity while walking along and looking down, almost like radar." Richard says he often used nothing but a large screwdriver to dig for relics. His table of artifacts is simply divided by which side of the creek his finds came from. "Keep it simple" is his mantra.

He says the natives who visited the area were stream based and made good use of the variety of plants that grew along the creek and its tributaries. Generations of these nomads came back over and over for centuries. Dating the points by size and shape is something he learned in his archaeology studies. When he picks up the artifacts, he casually says this is a thousand years old; that could be four or six thousand years old. "Where I am personally right now it is not so different from the people who visited this place over and over. I wanted to come back here to be a part of this land and the creek again. This landscape can heal people. and it has taken care of them for a long, long time." Susan agrees: "This is a binding place."

The quarter mile of Barton Creek on the Starks' property snakes beside busy two-lane Bell Springs Road. In recent years the area has attracted wedding venues and wineries, subdivisions, and country estates far grander than the Starks' place. When Richard Sr. and Susan bought the land in 1969, Bell Springs Road off US 290 west of Dripping Springs was gravel. They had to drive across five cattle guards to get to their acreage. Both educators in Austin at the time, the Starks wanted to raise their two daughters and son in the country. To help pay for building a house, they started a summer day camp with ball fields and basic facilities. Sports Country Camp featured swimming, tennis, basketball, and football for youths seven to thirteen. The family moved onto the property in

Richard and Susan Stark raised their family and ran a youth camp on the creek.

1976. Richard became principal of Dripping Springs Elementary in 1980 and retired in 1995. Susan taught school for five years before raising her kids.

"There were no structures here when we bought the land. We had everything built and did the taping and floating for walls ourselves," Susan says on my first visit in 2016 just a year after the couple closed the camp for good. "We did it all at the camp, from teaching kids to cook and playing music to outdoor science and the sports."

"The first year we were here, we decided to have swimming lessons in the creek," Richard Sr. told a reporter for the *Austin American-Statesman* in 1982. "But it was mostly dry, and Susan, who was going to be the instructor, said no way." (An L-shaped pool was built for lessons, though campers would continue to jump in the creek to cool off.) "How much we use the creek depends so much on the rainfall," Richard Sr. continued in the article, pointing to a small fern-lined waterfall. "Some summers this is just like a horseshoe falls. It's really pretty. I'm told that a church in town used to do all their baptisms here."

In recent years, two droughts left the Starks' stretch of the creek with only enough water to barely sit in let alone go for a swim. The nearest strong spring is downstream of their land and across the road. That creek property was the site of another camp in the 1940s. Camp Ah-wah-nee had a swimming hole, cabins, and Sunday services atop a hill overlooking the creek. Susan says she and Richard liked the idea that their Sports Country Camp continued the area's history of exposing young people to the natural world. Wild turkeys and deer are drawn to the creek. Sunfish, bass, and perch grow to fishing pole–worthy size in wet years. As we talk, Barton Creek is full, flowing, and photogenic, tucked into the shade of mature sycamore, walnut, and elm trees. The bottomland along the creek is noticeably cooler and restful. While the water is seldom more than three or four feet deep where it pools, the Starks say they have seen days of rainstorms turn the creek into a frothing river a hundred feet across.

Travis Dalrymple was a camper at Sports Country for six years beginning in 1989 and stayed on for two decades as a counselor and eventually camp director. "It was how camp is supposed be with no A/C, no videos or iPhones. Kids learning sports, fishing, playing tennis, being one with nature and the Earth. One year we had massive rains, and the creek got so high that we built a big raft just to learn how to do it. It floated eight girls before it sank. I used to catch bass and perch in my off-hours in what was always an amazing creek out there." Dalrymple, a teacher and tennis coach at Westwood High School in Round Rock, keeps in touch with some of the campers and adds that "friendships made there will last forever."

The Starks closed Sports Country Camp after forty-four summers of hard work. The program grew to a residential summer camp that accommodated up to fifty youths and fourteen counselors. "We chose on purpose to stay small," says Richard Sr., comparing their camp to some of the Hill Country camps that serve several hundred youths each summer. The couple never wanted a place with too many modern conveniences. They didn't have air-conditioning in their open-beamed, rambling house until the 1990s. I try to imagine the summers when kids filled the long camp dormitory that still held rows of bunkbeds and mattresses on my first visit. An octagonal gaga ball pit is nearby, and four basketball hoops hang inside a dark barn-wood structure. A drawing on one wall features branches and a trunk labeled the Sports Country Family Tree, with the signatures of campers from 1979 on. When I return a year later, the dismantling of the camp is under way and the dormitory is now a comfortable place to sit and read.

Since 1998, a cozy, rustic cabin that backs up to the hillside above the creek is rented for weekend escapes. Susan makes breakfast for guests upon request, though she confesses she's happy if they don't want that. The small house, built cordwood style from cedar posts, is advertised as the Cabin on Barton Creek, a place for couples to "sit still to listen to the creek and watch the wildlife. Or, take your book down to the tree swing near the creek. Only the birds will interrupt." The Starks' rental cabin benefits from the growth of visitors to the area. They come from Austin for the quiet. Or they come for the plentiful nearby wedding venues and Dripping Springs' shops for people who roam the countryside to buy things.

"When we first moved out here, one of our neighbors was so territorial and wary of strangers that he

The Sports Country Camp near Dripping Springs spanned four decades of summers.

would take down the license plate numbers of people he didn't know who came down this road," says Susan. "It's a barrage of cars and limos now. These people going to and from wherever need to be careful. They are unfamiliar with how quickly the road crossing at Barton Creek can flood. Schoolhouse Creek, the tributary closer to town, goes over the road sometimes, too."

Her son, Richard, says development on and around Barton Creek could have been so much greater had it not been for the political uprising around the time of his now-legendary hike. As we wind up our visit, we talk about how a land ethic for Austin was created then. "People realized they needed to buy water-protection land in the urban shadow," Richard says. "They did that and it's made a difference."

Truman Breed Jr. didn't have far to walk to school for first grade since the one-room Bell Springs School was on his parents' land off West Fitzhugh Road. Five students were taught there by one teacher. After school on hot days, Truman and his younger brother and sister, Benny and Wanda, often headed to a shaded swimming hole on Barton Creek. Less than a mile upstream of where the Starks live, the creek runs through 1,400 acres of pastures and hills that Truman's father bought from several owners in the early 1930s. His father, also named Truman, and his mother, Allene, had been living in Dripping Springs seven miles to the south. The ranch gave them the opportunity to raise sheep and goats and plenty of acreage for the kids to explore.

But before Truman could move up to second grade, his father died from a brain tumor. Allene needed to support the family, so they moved to Austin, where she was hired at Austin National Bank. She would work there for many years as secretary to the bank president. The land and its nearly mile-long stretch of Barton Creek drew Truman back for visits as often as he could. His grandfather on his mother's side owned a Dripping Springs gas station, where Truman filled up cars and trucks on weekends. In the summer when school was out, he climbed on a Greyhound bus out of downtown Austin on Sunday afternoons and stayed for days with his grandparents in town. They frequently drove out to the ranch. "I had a horse out

Truman Breed's father bought rolling acreage on Barton Creek in the 1930s.

here named Sunny, and I would ride the heck out of her bareback in the pasture. I tried roping goats on her, but I was never very good at it," Truman tells me as we sit on the front porch of his house overlooking a pond stocked with catfish.

As young adults, Truman and his siblings drew straws to divide up ownership of the land. Wanda got the old ranch place where Truman had grown up. Benny got cleared pastureland. Truman got 350 acres—the best part in his estimation—with the longest stretch of Barton Creek and the pristine swimming hole at a waterfall. "My mother could have sold the land, but she wanted to keep it for her family. I'll always be grateful and thankful for her doing that," says Truman, now in his eighties. We take in views of the hills sloping down to the creek from the one-story house he moved onto the property.

Truman, who lives in Austin, says his grown children and grandchildren use the comfortable, rambling house whenever they want. The original part of the house once sat behind a grocery store on West 29th Street near the University of Texas campus. Truman bought it and the store when he was a commercial land officer at Austin National Bank. He was ready to try something different.

"I always liked tools, and I was a pretty good craftsman working with my hands. At the bank, I was the youngest and the lowest-paid loan officer. So, when a fella came by who wanted to sell his hardware business, I told him I'd buy it. I wanted to get into business for myself." The store became the first location of Breed and Company, a hardware and home goods emporium known for personable and experienced service. "I took it from $250,000 a year in sales to several million dollars. I taught my staff that when someone came in the door, you didn't wait to ask if they needed help." In 2015, after his son Greg Breed helped expand the company to three stores while fighting competition from the big hardware chains, the business was sold.

Nowadays, Truman nurses his collection of old wood planers at the ranch house and directs workers who gradually are clearing the land of cedar trees crowding out native oaks and grasses. "Little rascals" is what he calls the cedars that spread out their roots close to the surface and quickly multiply. The shaded soil around thick stands of cedars becomes barren and easily erodes. We take a drive around the ranch and stop downstream from the family swimming hole. Barton Creek makes an elbow bend around a hundred-foot limestone bluff here. Facing the hill is what's left of the 1855 home of Pleasant and Elizabeth Alexander and their two children. The grand, five-room house was built with squared-off blocks of stone quarried from the banks of the creek. The ten-foot-high walls remain remarkably intact today, but the roof is long gone.

Truman points out a corner room with no doorway to the rest of the house. He says the room probably was for travelers needing a place to spend the night. Behind the house is a large field where the Alexanders raised food for their family and farm animals. Originally from Tennessee, Alexander and his wife are buried in a tiny fenced cemetery across the field. Truman has kept the two tombstones standing, but the weathered, simple inscriptions are difficult to read: "P. D. Alexander—died 1883" and "E. M. Alexander—died 1891."

An account of the Alexander family's history was written by J. Marie Bassett of the Hays County Historical Commission in 2016. Her research found that Pleasant Duke Alexander arrived in Texas by 1836 and served with Col. Ed Burleson's volunteer force that put down insurrections in the Republic of Texas in 1839 and 1842. Alexander received a land grant during that time and settled in Bastrop County, marrying Elizabeth Margaret Bull in 1843. The Alexanders lived there until they moved farther west in 1855, buying 131 acres of fertile land on Barton Creek, where they built their house.

Pleasant became involved in Hays County politics and was appointed county judge in 1867, serving until 1878. He also was a trustee of the Collins School on Barton Creek, which started in 1876 with thirteen pupils. By 1880, according to the census that year, Pleasant's son Stephen was overseeing the farm and his father was suffering from consumption (tuberculosis). After the deaths of their parents, the son moved to Arizona and his sister moved into Austin. They sold the land, which traded hands a few times before it and more acreage was bought by the Breeds.

As Greg Breed drives us up a steep, rocky road to the top of the bluff overlooking the ruins of the Alexanders' house, Truman talks about helping a ranch hand dig up the smaller cedar trees with a Bobcat to burn them. He also hired a company to bring in an eight-foot-wide "cedar eater" to chew up large cedars and leave mulch behind with minimal land disturbance. "I heard that in the distant past there were no cedars out here, but they came in strong before I was born," Truman says. "You cut those things down and then see a new sprout nearby in no time."

The Breeds' ranch, which no longer is used for grazing, now is a paradise for quail. Greg puts out milo for the quail, and protein feed goes to the deer. No hunting is allowed. "Every three or four years the county is supposed to send someone out to check on what we are doing for our wildlife valuation, but they haven't been out for a long time," he says. "I call the office, and they say they are too busy and behind on inspections."

Our drive around the land continues as Truman directs us to a sprawling grove of stately oaks with canopies darkening the old farm road through it. "My mother called this the enchanted forest," he says in a wistful voice as we enter the quiet grove. Next up is the swimming hole where Truman has cooled himself through eight decades. Barton Creek widens to about thirty-five feet here, much of it shaded by sycamore and other trees along the banks. Water flows steadily over a natural dam of rock ledges. A small concrete pad with a barbecue pit just above the creek serves as a place to picnic and leave clothing. "Nobody ever swam here in a bathing suit," Truman claims with a chuckle. "It's my favorite place on the ranch. It was a great spot to bring a girlfriend."

The memories are good ones, but the Breeds look to the future as well. "I'm afraid of what will happen in this whole area of Barton Creek if everything is sold off piecemeal," says Greg. "I hope my kids will see this land as something sacred and holy for the family. My grandmother sacrificed a lot to keep it."

The family swimming hole is a place of memories for Truman and son Greg Breed.

FAMILY LANDS : **33**

4 PUBLIC BATTLES

Barton Springs Uprising Stokes Decades of Political and Legal Fights

It is unimaginable today. But not on June 7, 1990. After several hours of regular business, the Austin City Council opened a public hearing on a zoning case at 4:30 p.m. It did not end until thirteen and a half hours later. Some eight hundred people—old and young, professionals and slackers, environmentalists and developers, lawyers on all sides, regular swimmers at Barton Springs Pool—walked to the dais one after another to say how they felt about a development plan for four thousand acres on six miles of Barton Creek.

The scene inside the modest council chambers at 307 W. Second Street was orderly as citizens lined up to speak. Mayor Lee Cooke called their names from a stack of index cards, and one by one the speakers who signed up were allotted three minutes to give their opinion or testimony. No protest signs were allowed inside, but plenty were waved outside on the narrow sidewalk as vehicles cruised by and drivers honked in support. Television and radio news crews broadcast from the chambers, drawing even more people to the hearing. Unlike inside today's architecturally grand and multistory City Hall, the chambers then were squeezed into a plain, cramped building several blocks from the main city offices. Liberty Lunch, a former lumberyard–turned–music club a few doors down, became a staging area for speakers and protesters waiting their turn inside the chambers.

The long night became known as the Barton Springs Uprising, though it wasn't the first time that citizens had stood up to the growth rush in Austin. There had been fights against a Barton Skyway bridge over the creek, a massive mall just above the creek, MoPac Expressway's southern plunge over the Edwards Aquifer recharge zone, and a Motorola plant in the aquifer's contributing zone. All were battles lost by environmentalists except for stopping the bridge in Barton Hills that would have linked South Lamar Boulevard and MoPac. The difference in the summer of 1990 was a City Council that was listening, a history of recent closings of Barton Springs Pool, and a focused agenda to save the creek from an outsider corporation. The night became a kickoff to lawsuits, moratoriums, new development ordinances, endangered species campaigns, bond issues for purchasing conservation lands and easements, Austin-bashing bills by the legislature, and creation of new city departments to protect the watersheds.

Uprisings often have a trigger event, and the decision over the Barton Creek Planned Unit Development (PUD) was it. Negotiations between city staff and

An all-night Austin City Council hearing in 1990 halted a massive development. (Photo by Alan Pogue)

developers of the PUD had produced several drafts of the agreement, the last finished late the night before the hearing. Austan Librach, director of environmental services for the city, was called on by the mayor to provide an overview before citizens spoke.

"Barton Creek in our view is currently impacted by pollution," he said, noting algae growth and sediment and nutrient increases where the PUD build-out would greatly expand the existing Barton Creek Country Club and Estates at Barton Creek. Librach defended the goals of the city's 1986 Comprehensive Watershed Ordinance but said its structural, buffer zone and erosion controls had not prevented degradation of the creek by the development built in the mid-1980s. "We cannot ensure that no degradation will occur in Barton Springs or the creek. Pollution levels for individual projects will increase two to eight times over baseline in some situations," he said. He predicted that Barton Springs Pool could be closed for more days as a result.

Librach's warning lit a fuse that citizens would keep burning through the night. Before the public took their shots at the development, Jim Bob Moffett spoke as chairman and CEO of Freeport-McMoRan, an international mining and drilling company with a real estate arm called FM Properties. His plan would add to the Estates of Barton Creek three thousand homes and apartments, three million square feet of commercial buildings, and three more golf courses on the property in the contributing zone of the Edwards Aquifer.

The former University of Texas football player from Houston began by attacking the *Austin Chronicle* weekly for its articles reporting the company's pollution record in the United States and Indonesia. A front-page illustration showed a closed Barton Springs Pool with the headline "If You Don't Read This Issue, We'll Poison Barton Springs." He said he was "dismayed by the malice" and portrayed himself as the rescuer of the property from financial ruins and small-tract subdividing. Indeed, a development company under former Texas governor John Connally and former lieutenant governor Ben Barnes had gone bankrupt and lost the land it planned to develop as an adjunct to its Estates project. Loans the Barnes-Connally company held were caught up in the savings and loan collapses of the late 1980s. Moffett acknowledged what he described as the "emotion" in the room and promised "we have done everything to ensure the safety of Barton Creek. And as a geologist, I can promise you I know more about Barton Creek than anyone in this room." Laughs and hoots followed, as did an admonition from the mayor against such outbursts.

Then a parade of the developers' experts testified about how well Barton Creek would be protected in the project. One was a Dallas ornithologist who said he was shown photos of the PUD's set-aside acreage that could become habitat for the golden-cheeked warbler. He admitted he had never laid eyes on Barton Creek or the land. Residents of the Estates of Barton Creek stated that they believed the PUD would bring in good neighbors. Environmental lawyer Bill Bunch stepped up to the lectern as one of the first speakers against the project. He cited the dismal environmental record of Freeport-McMoRan in this country and abroad. He described evidence of Barton Creek running murky downstream of the Estates and clear upstream of it. He said he asked for but received no data about the pesticides, fertilizers, and sewage effluent applied to the present Estates' golf course. "We've asked the important question. Is [the PUD] going to protect the creek? Is it going to protect Barton Springs? We have the answer, and that answer is no." He concluded by mocking the developers' contention that they would be a partner with the city in their project. "Do not be an accomplice to the death of Barton Creek, and do not be an accomplice to the death of Barton Springs."

Following him was an array of opponents who included University of Texas students, mothers of kids who swam in Barton Springs, a former United Nations water-quality worker, a speaker parodying the developers' claim that "we're gonna make the creek better than mama nature made it," a poet pleading respect for the spirit of the springs, and a self-described "uninvolved, nonvoter" asking for her taxes to be raised if necessary to take the place of city revenues from the development. All took their three minutes at the microphone one by one through the night and into the morning. Shannon Sedwick, entertainer-in-chief of Esther's Follies, sang to the tune of "Cry Me a River" about Barton Creek turning from blue to brown and don't let the people of Austin down.

At the time of the PUD hearing, Bill Bunch and his then-wife Helen Ballew (who had worked at The Nature Conservancy on land protection) had recently started the Hill Country Foundation, a new environmental group. A San Antonio native, Bill was a 1986 graduate of the University of California at Berkeley law school with a bachelor's degree in environmental biology from the University of Colorado. He had helped get out the word about the hearing and knew the development fight would be a test of Austin's commitment to protecting its natural treasures from rapid growth. What he didn't know is how fast and furious the political battles would be played out over the next two decades.

Since the late 1960s when the Austin Environmental Council formed as an umbrella group for civic groups and local chapters of the Sierra Club and Audubon Society, Austinites were wary and weary of uncontrolled growth. The environmental council successfully fought the city's subsidizing of development with rebates to builders for their water and sewer lines. In the wake of the first national Earth Day in 1970, other organizations started: We Care Austin, the Zilker Park Posse, Save Barton Creek Association, Earth First, Clean Water Action, and more. The city created an Office of Environmental Resources Management and hired as its first director Stuart Henry, a Houston attorney with environmental credentials. Henry later formed his own environmental law firm and hired the young Bill Bunch.

Protection of the city's many creeks became an immediate issue. Barton Creek on the south and Bull Creek on the north were battlegrounds as developers pushed for sewer lines in the channels as the lowest-cost way to serve their new subdivisions. The growth debates are aptly described by William S. Swearingen Jr., a St. Edward's University professor, in his 2010 book *Environmental City*:

> The conflict emerged when people who wanted to retain their quality of life began to try to direct growth and save some of the natural environment during the time that Austin was becoming a big city. The quality-of-life people defined Austin as a place that was pleasant to live in because of its natural environment—the hills, the river, the creeks. They wanted to preserve, use, and enjoy those environmental features in their daily life—to walk in the creeks, see the hills, feel the water. They were beginning to define Austin as a place that was built into and defined by those features, and they began to promote the idea that growth should be guided in order to save those features.
>
> But the idea of slower, more deliberate, and controlled growth that preserved the natural environment conflicted with ideas about growth for profit held by land speculators and many business people. Those competing desires created the conflicts that have been fought out in city politics, lawsuits, and rulemaking for four decades, from the late 1960s until today.

Sitting on the south lawn of Barton Springs Pool in the fall of 2017, Bill Bunch, executive director of the Save Our Springs Alliance, tries to recall details of the long night of the 1990 PUD hearing. He was there the whole time, not representing a client but as a citizen involved with the Save Barton Creek Association and the local Sierra Club. "I remember I fell asleep for a little while stretched out on some chairs I put together in the basement of the chamber. I had spoken early in the evening."

Attorney Bill Bunch's environmental battles continue today on many fronts.

He laughs about Jim Bob Moffett's claim that Moffett knew more about Barton Creek than anyone. And laughs again at the theatrics of Robert H. Dedman, whose ClubCorp had built the golf country club on the creek and was partnering with Freeport-McMoRan for more courses surrounded by houses. Dedman recited lines from Longfellow and a Rudyard Kipling poem: "If you can keep your head when all about you / Are losing theirs and blaming it on you. / If you can trust yourself when all men doubt you. . . ."

Bill credits radio ads bought by the environmental groups and KUT deejays for urging the public to attend the hearing. But he says he had no idea the turnout would create an all-nighter. "There were a lot of new faces there, and those people said some amazing things. The absolute best statement I remember is not on the video because the guy spoke when the tape was being changed. He was off-the-charts hilarious and dead on as well." Exactly what that speaker said or who he was is lost in Bill's memory, but the lawyer says what made the hearing so dynamic was people like that who were not representing any group.

"I would have spent hours and hours studying the details and documents of a case like this, but some of these people who spoke came up with things I hadn't thought of. The wisdom of that crowd was incredibly powerful." Bill and others counted the votes on the council before the hearing. "We knew we were going to lose, with five of the seven council members against us." He was wrong. The council vote at the end of the long night was unanimous to deny the development permit. The crowd and their thoughtful, impassioned pleas won out.

After defeat of the Barton Creek PUD, the environmental groups turned their sights toward stopping other developers and waivers from the city's Comprehensive Watershed Ordinance. The City Council enacted a four-month moratorium on new development in the Barton Creek watershed a few months after the uprising. But then the May 1991 council elections resulted in a pro-development majority that slowed and weakened a rewrite of the water-quality ordinance. Meanwhile, Barton Springs Pool repeatedly closed after high fecal coliform bacteria counts.

Environmentalists were outraged by the closings and the council's obstructions. The Save Our Springs Coalition, cofounded by Bill Bunch and Brigid Shea of the Clean Water Action group, led a petition drive that produced thirty thousand signatures demanding a restrictive SOS Ordinance be put on the May 1992 ballot. The council refused. The coalition filed suit, and an appeals court ordered the council to hold an election on the citizens' initiative. The vote on August 8, 1992, approved the SOS Ordinance by a 2–1 margin. The new regulations strictly limited impervious cover in the Barton Springs zone of the Edwards Aquifer and mandated that runoff from developments be as clean as it was prior to construction.

Bill was heavily involved in the team effort that drafted the ordinance, but he was surprised by the margin of the vote. "I was still a political newbie then. Senior political advisers, including David Butts and Mark Yznaga, had done the polling. They knew we were going to win, but they didn't tell us because they wanted us to work our asses off shaking every voter out of the trees before the polls closed." On the same ballot as the ordinance was a $22 million bond proposal to buy lands for habitat protection of endangered birds and cave-dwelling invertebrate species. The acreage was the first step in the Balcones Canyonlands Conservation Plan (BCCP) to create a network of city, county, and federal conservation lands. The 1992 ballot also included $20 million in bonds for the Wilderness Park to extend the Barton Creek greenbelt. All three measures passed overwhelmingly. Six years later, voters would approve water-rate increases to raise $65 million for fifteen thousand acres of conservation land to protect water quality.

Bill was on the seventeen-member committee that crafted the Balcones plan as an agreement between environmentalists and developers to set aside habitat lands in return for easing restrictions on developable acreage. He voted against the plan when it became apparent the amount of protected habitat would be scaled back from 125,000 acres to less than 60,000 and much of it would be fragmented. His critics cite that as an example of his fierce unwillingness to compromise. Bill says today the leadership of the BCCP committee at the time "rolled over" and was "spooked by developers."

Following the heady days of the Barton Springs Uprising and passage of the SOS Ordinance and conservation bonds, a hurricane aimed at the city with court cases, turnovers of elected officials, "Austin bashing" by the Texas legislature, scientific studies, and pollution problems. The era of the development wars was full on. When I look at a time line of those events and more, it makes my head spin at how furiously battles involving the Edwards Aquifer, the Barton Creek watershed, and its springs unfolded.

The legislature enacted its first "grandfathering" law in 1987 to shield developers from new water-quality regulations after permit applications had been filed. Thus, the lawmakers' reaction to the SOS Ordinance was not unexpected in 1993, and they passed a bill to invalidate the ordinance. "We knew that was coming, so we incorporated as the SOS Defense Fund soon after the vote to fight for the ordinance in court," Bill tells me. "Developer money was buying influence in the legislature. They weren't going to screw us publicly after the ordinance vote, but they knew they could do it privately." Nor were the environmentalists surprised that developers earlier had filed numerous permit applications before city voters approved the SOS Ordinance. In the three months leading up to the vote, 239 applications were filed to ensure their plans would be covered by less restrictive regulations.

Governor Ann Richards told a reporter she would sign the anti-SOS bill, but a political adviser for city activists talked to her that night at a dinner and convinced her otherwise. "She called the reporter back and said she had changed her mind. It was that kind of crazy stuff," Bill says. Her veto message as the 1993 legislature closed was simple: "This bill would allow most development in the Barton Creek watershed in Travis County to escape regulation under the City of Austin's water-quality ordinances. It would undermine the results of the

1992 local election in which voters overwhelmingly approved a new water-quality ordinance."

In the spring of 1994, a type of algae was found in the pool that scientists said was the result of fertilizers in runoff. The US Fish and Wildlife Service had recently proposed putting the Barton Springs salamander on the endangered species list. By the end of the year, a study of the Edwards Aquifer found higher-than-normal concentrations of bacteria, sediment, hydrocarbons, pesticides, and arsenic. Developers and landowners, meanwhile, prepared for another round of battles in the 1995 legislative session. This time Richards would not be a veto threat, defeated after one term by Republican George W. Bush.

Another pushback to Austin environmentalists had arrived in 1994 in the form of Marshall E. Kuykendall, a tall Texan with a family history going back to Stephen F. Austin's colony. He grew up among the springs and sinks of Onion Creek on a Hays County ranch that once covered eleven thousand acres. When Austin and Travis County officials—and briefly Richards—supported environmental groups seeking a federal designation of the entire Barton Creek watershed as an Outstanding National Resource Water, Marshall had heard enough of what sounded to him like unlawful private property takings by the government. Then the US Fish and Wildlife Service proposed vast preserves for golden-cheeked warbler protection. He fired back, organizing a group he called Take Back Texas to get a state property rights bill passed. His come-and-take-it cannon shot against the environmentalists was a march of three thousand supporters up Congress Avenue to the Capitol.

The Private Real Property Rights Preservation Act was passed by the 1995 legislature that purported to answer the pleas of Take Back Texas. But it included sweeping exemptions, including municipalities, and set a high bar of 25 percent devaluation of land by government action before compensation would be paid. Marshall resigned to let someone else carry on Take Back Texas. Nearly twenty-five years later, Marshall still has the swagger of a man whose voice was heard, even if for a brief, intense time. Now he enjoys writing stories about colorful characters and visiting the sites of old frontier forts when he's not regaling a group of fellow coffee drinkers every morning in a Dripping Springs café. I meet him there to ask about Take Back Texas but also to find out what he thinks about developers' plans in the area. "I'm not a developer," he cautions. "I broker the sale of ranches, and I'm very conservative because I love the land."

Of his long-ago involvement in legislative politics, Marshall says he was "angry for about a minute." But he still scoffs at what he sees as assaults on private property rights for the sake of birds and salamanders. Marshall says he opposed conservation easements for a while because they are "very difficult decisions by families to take an estate away from future generations in perpetuity. But I'm not opposed now. I think they're fabulous if that's what a landowner wants to do." Part of his family's former ranch in the Edwards Aquifer recharge zone was sold to an owner who later put the property under a City of Austin conservation easement known as the Onion Creek Management Unit.

As the wrangling between city and state officials

Marshall Kuykendall rallied landowners for 1995 property-rights legislation.

continued at the 1997 session, the legislature inadvertently repealed the grandfathering law. The following year, the Texas Supreme Court upheld the SOS Ordinance, citing such regulations as "a nationally recognized method of preserving water quality" and recognizing that the city "has the right to significantly limit development in watershed areas." The same month as the 1998 Supreme Court decision, Austin voters approved a proposition to acquire about fifteen thousand acres of water-protection land in the Barton Creek watershed. More acreage would come under conservation easements through The Nature Conservancy and the Hill Country Conservancy.

Asked about success in steering development to other, less environmentally sensitive parts of the city, Bill Bunch says that "one of the best examples often overlooked now was Silicon Labs. They started out on one of FM Properties' tracts off Southwest Parkway, but when they wanted to expand with another building and were close to inking a deal with the developer out there, they reversed course and moved downtown to the two former Computer Sciences Corp. buildings. They would tell you it is one of the best things they ever did to get out of the Barton Creek watershed and move downtown."

Not that further development in that area along Southwest Parkway stopped. Other high-tech buildings, luxury apartments, and condos have been built in recent years. The big swath of green behind them is the forty-one hundred acres of The Nature Conservancy's owned and managed Barton Creek Habitat Preserve. Across the parkway, a 325,000-square-foot commercial development of shops and a movie theater opened in 2018.

Bill's intolerance for compromise was tested in 1999 when Austin mayor Kirk Watson convened meetings of the Austin Chamber of Commerce, the Real Estate Council of Austin, and environmental leaders. The idea was to call a truce, talk, and figure out how to avoid battles in courts and at the legislature. Bill lasted only the first day. "There were some negotiations on deal making that I didn't have the stomach for," he says. "The only tangible thing that came out of it was the incorporation of the Hill Country Conservancy.

Protest graffiti takes over a Barton Creek watershed development's sign in 2017.

We realized we needed a land trust that would expand private land protection."

Throughout the decade, development in Austin continued unabated despite economic downturns, bankruptcies, and the morphing of companies, including Freeport-McMoRan, into other entities. The Barton Creek PUD eventually was completed under the grandfathered development plans after mitigation agreements to set aside conservation acreage elsewhere. The sprawling Circle C subdivision south of Austin over the recharge zone changed hands several times and finally was built out with twelve thousand people and annexed by the city.

George Cofer, an Austin native and executive director of the Hill Country Conservancy for nearly twenty years, regales me with stories during a long afternoon at his house:

> I remember getting very irritated with people saying we can build all this stuff on the creek without harming the springs. So I began working for free at first with the Save Our Springs Coalition. Then I heard [Texas Agriculture Commissioner] Jim Hightower was bringing Robert Redford to town for a reelection campaign event of his. Knowing Redford's history of swimming at Barton Springs, I pleaded with Jim to let us have him, too. He did and we sold a whole lot of hundred-dollar tickets for a fund-raiser of ours. Somehow, because of that fluke, it was perceived I knew about raising money. [Redford learned to swim at Barton Springs Pool as a boy visiting his grandparents in Austin. The actor was filmed poolside in the 2007 documentary *The Unforeseen* as he talked about the value of such environmental gems.]
>
> So that's what I did from then on. But we didn't stop Barton Creek Estates and Jim Bob Moffett. After three years of our lives fighting that, sleeping on the floors of SOS, I had an epiphany that I needed to try some other strategies and do something else with my life. . . .
>
> We have been trying to figure out over the past twenty years, and are still trying, how to balance the

Clark Hancock provides an Edwards Aquifer lesson at Barton Springs University day.

extraordinary growth with at least some green infrastructure. We'll never be able to set aside land fast enough. Very few landowners are willing to give up their development rights because the offers are so extraordinary. There's land out there now flipping for twenty thousand dollars an acre. It's just crazy. The big picture is that these cats with money from out of Austin, out of state, and even from other countries don't understand that there isn't going to be enough water. They just don't get that. In my opinion, one reason the Save Our Springs Alliance is not as effective as it used to be is that the courts and Fish and Wildlife do not have the political backing they once had. So it becomes an educational issue for us to talk about the salamanders and birds.

David Hillis, integrative biology professor at the University of Texas, was fascinated with salamanders when he first lived in Austin in the 1970s and then studied them when he returned in the 1980s after graduate school. He soon found himself immersed in political battles over the population of salamanders in Barton Springs hanging on by a thread in their critical habitat. To rescue them, Hillis aimed for the Endangered Species Act, which protected any species likely to become extinct throughout all or a large part of its range. The act required detailed studies but also needed to have public support. The answer, he said in a 2016 presentation to young future scientists at the University of Texas Environmental Science Institute, was a local education campaign with salamander T-shirts, Frisbees, and cartoon renditions to personalize the aquatic, seldom-seen critter.

By 1990, the cause of ensuring that Barton Springs would be fit for people and salamanders through future generations coalesced after repeated closings of the pool because of high coliform counts. A federal petition to list the salamander as an endangered species was filed after Hillis, Paul Chippendale, and Andrew Price wrote a scientific paper describing and naming the Barton Springs salamander. The US Fish and Wildlife Service gave preliminary approval to the salamander as a protected new species in 1993. But two years later Governor Bush requested a delay in the listing and US Secretary of the Interior Bruce Babbitt said his agency would withdraw its proposal to protect the salamander.

The next step by Fish and Wildlife was a review by a panel of experts with no Texas scientists as members. Hillis testified at the agency's hearing and then listened as panelist and biologist Vic Hutchison of the University of Oklahoma concluded, "In my opinion, the Barton Springs salamander is the most endangered species of vertebrate in the United States." Nonetheless, Babbitt refused to list the salamander in July 1996. The Save Our Springs Alliance quickly filed suit against the Department of Interior, claiming Babbitt "had bowed to politics and ignored science." In March 1997, a federal judge ruled the agency had violated federal law by not basing its decision solely on the best scientific data. On April 30, after four years of battles, the salamander finally was listed as an endangered species.

Today, the Barton Springs salamander "is the most-studied salamander in the world," Hillis told his audience of young students. Population numbers for the salamander have recovered, although the counts vary widely between wet and dry cycles. In 2013, the Austin blind salamander was listed as endangered as well after it was identified as a distinct species. In the spirit of Hillis's talks, a one-day Barton Springs University was started in 2015 to educate high school students about the salamanders and other local environmental issues. The free "classes," demonstrations, and displays by the Save Barton Creek Association and other groups each September also focus on the Edwards Aquifer and water-protection and conservation lands. Organized by the city parks and water-protection departments and the SOS Alliance, the program buses students to Barton Springs and invites the public to learn about water quality and usage from the people who battle daily on behalf of Austin's environment. The university day once a year is a fun outdoor learning event that increasingly draws adults and youths beyond the selected high school groups.

Another fun factor keeping attention on Austin's environmental treasures is Bill Oliver, who bills himself as MrHabitat. For many years the troubadour has been singing his original songs about Barton Springs and other issues. Oliver is a staple at Save Barton Creek Association events and he presents his entertaining programs at area schools.

As the 2000s arrived, Austin and out-of-state developers aimed at lands to the southwest of Circle C in the Onion Creek watershed and around Dripping Springs and Bee Cave in the Barton Creek watershed. The Lower Colorado River Authority (LCRA) decided to build a pipeline out US 290 into northern Hays County after longtime residents pleaded for help with their wells going dry. The LCRA already had the Uplands Water Treatment Plant off Bee Caves Road to process raw water pumped from Lake Austin.

The SOS Alliance and SBCA reacted quickly, seeking a preliminary injunction in federal court to stop LCRA's plans until environmental impact studies could be done. In a negotiated settlement with LCRA that followed the injunction denial, the authority agreed that developments built using the new water supply would limit impervious cover and treat runoff. "A mistake we made in that was focusing more on nonpoint source runoff standards and not on how wastewater would be treated," says Bill Bunch. Most of the new developments rely on their own package treatment plants for sewage.

He says the number-one problem upstream in the Barton Creek watershed is these wastewater treatment facilities. "Because these plants are 'no discharge,' they don't have to get a permit under the federal Clean Water Act. Mostly they operate as indirect discharge plants that treat the wastewater to some level and then irrigate with it over a pasture or golf course or what have you. The soils and plants assimilate the water, but over time the waste remains. It's better than direct discharge, in theory, but almost always these plants are not operated properly. They put these machines on autopilot and there's nobody there. When the soil gets saturated, the permit says they're not allowed to irrigate, but then equipment breaks and stays broken for weeks. So instead of spreading the wastewater out over say fifty acres, it winds up just on ten or fifteen acres. Then you start getting channelized flow into creek tributaries."

There are now good data from US Geological Survey and City of Austin research, Bill says, "that treated wastewater from those package plants is getting in the creeks, coming down Barton Creek, Onion Creek, and Bear Creek and getting into the aquifer and then coming back out at Barton Springs." SOS Alliance continues to fight settlement of Dripping Springs' request for a state permit to discharge treated effluent from its wastewater plant into a tributary of Onion Creek. Bill was not satisfied with a $72 million bond issue for conservation land on an Austin ballot in 2018. "Voters approved $65 million in 1998, and now our appraised tax value in the city is at least more than double what it was then. Land is a lot more expensive now, so we need more bond money."

We wind down our discussion at Barton Springs so Bill can get in a swim. I ask where his future battles will be focused. Without hesitating, he talks about fighting plans for more and bigger roads over the aquifer. "There is a lot of political upheaval right now over toll roads and transportation issues. Hopefully, we'll slow all that road building down long enough for people to realize that technology is going to help us use the pavement we have now a lot more efficiently. Then we won't have to spend literally billions of dollars to pave the watershed to serve development we don't want to see in the first place."

5 SHIELD RANCH

Six Miles and Sixty-Eight Hundred Acres of Protected Water and Land

An overgrown footpath lined with flowering bushes curves around one side of the old family house on the Shield Ranch west of Austin. It is an inviting place for wildlife on an overcast summer morning. Photographer Alberto Martinez strolls along the path looking for a scenic spot to shoot a portrait of the matriarch of the Shield-Ayres family and her son, daughter, and a grandson. As the family waits inside, I ask them about their long-considered decision to put a conservation easement on the ranch in the late 1990s.

Alberto turns to walk back the way he had come. A three-foot-long diamondback rattler is in his way. Stepping back, he instinctively lifts his camera to shoot a few frames before heading into the house to tell us about the visitor. We all hurry out, including Patricia Shield Ayres, in her mid-eighties. No one in the family seems particularly alarmed—one more snake on a sixty-eight hundred–acre ranch of wildness encircling six miles of Barton Creek. A ranch hand arrives a few minutes later with a bucket and snake stick. The reptile has retreated under some bushes but is found and snared as we listen to its rattling protests. After the worker buckets the snake for a trip to a more remote part of the property, the family walks to the backyard for a portrait beneath a sprawling old oak. Patricia; son, Robert (Bob) Atlee Ayres; daughter, Vera Ayres Bowen; and Vera's son Marshall Bowen all seem pleased that Alberto and I witnessed this small sampling of nature on their land. The Shield Ranch, after all, teems with things growing, flowing, scampering, and slithering. "It's been a good year for snakes," Patricia proclaims.

Midway on Barton Creek's journey from its source to the Colorado River in downtown Austin, the ranch is the largest conservation-easement property on the creek. And with nearly all its acreage in Travis County, the ranch may be the biggest privately owned conservation land in a metropolitan county of Texas. It is just west of tony Bee Cave and eleven miles north of Dripping Springs' town center. New subdivisions are creeping up Ranch Road 12 and Hamilton Pool Road almost to the ranch's modest main gate. But after I drive into the ranch, I feel like I'm in another century. The ranch is immense, with views of green hillsides, valleys, and pastures in every direction. Fed by springs and tributaries on the ranch, Barton Creek enjoys a quiet, refreshing respite here from population pressures and pollutants as it bisects the family land.

Shield Ranch master planners: Marshall Bowen, Patricia Ayres, Bob Ayres, and Vera Bowen.

Jeff Francell, director of land protection for The Nature Conservancy's office in Austin, says bringing the Shield Ranch under a conservation easement held by the conservancy was vital to the health of the creek in the late 1990s. The Shield-Ayres family continues to own all the land, but the easement prohibits development of the property in perpetuity. "The biggest thing that happened to protect Barton Creek was getting the Shield Ranch into a conservation easement. It sits right in the middle of the watershed, six thousand–plus acres and six miles of the creek on both sides," says Jeff. "That land does a lot to clean up the water on the way into town, and conversely, if it had been developed, it would do a terrible job and add a lot of pollution to the creek."

The family wanted to do something philanthropic, he says, but the land was a huge economic asset. To realize some money from the potential development value of the property, the family in 1999 sold to the City of Austin an easement relinquishing their development rights on 1,676 acres of the ranch. Six months earlier, the family had donated a conservation easement on 4,600 acres to The Nature Conservancy. Since those deals, 112 acres in perimeter tracts have been added to the ranch to stave off the building of gas stations and convenience stores to service nearby new residents. The entire ranch is managed by the family to protect native vegetation, wildlife, and the water that flows into and down Barton Creek. "This was the first time in Texas that there was a systematic program to purchase conservation easements. Now there are those kinds of purchases all across Texas," says Jeff.

Shield Ranch's backstory is one of wealth and perseverance. Money from oil paid for a natural treasure. The generations that followed figured out how to enhance and protect the land for the public and themselves. Forever. The modern era of the ranch began in 1938 when Patricia's parents, Fred W. and Vera Shield, bought the core acreage. The San Antonio family lived in the city but visited the ranch on weekends and stayed there through the summers. Patricia, an only child, began riding horses at an early age. "Mother would ride around the ranch, and I would accompany her. I'd also go out on horseback with the ranch hands to tend to the goats, sheep, and cattle. Dad raised quarter horses and cutting horses in the 1940s and '50s, including a prized stud named Shield's Traveler."

Deer and turkey are plentiful on the ranch, and Patricia learned to hunt here. I talk to the family's matriarch in a side room just beyond where a very large elk head stares out from above the living room fireplace. Patricia shot it at age sixteen on a backpacking trip into the Wyoming wilderness with her father. Barton Creek was a big part of her visits growing up. "We all loved the creek. We swam in the hole down from this house and another farther out that we called the Blue Hole. Our foreman, Horace Eckols, lived on the ranch with his wife, Lola, and family. They and their friends would load up a wagon with food and fishing gear, and we'd all go down to the Blue Hole to fish. Those were very memorable times for me catching bass and perch and catfish. Mother loved to fish."

Eckols worked the ranch from 1935, when electric power had not yet reached there, to his death in 1991. It was pretty much a condition of the ranch's sale to Fred Shield that Eckols and his family would stay on. Vera Bowen describes Eckols as a horticulturist who enjoyed gardening and cultivating. He planted a peach orchard and took pride in grafting the trees. He nurtured hundreds of pecan trees along the creek. Some of the native pecans grafted with improved varieties are still there, but others were abandoned to protect the creek from the fertilizers and pesticides they required. The canning of preserves—peaches, wild plums and grapes, and agarita berries—was a family tradition that Patricia passed on to Vera and Bob.

Marshall, a third-year student at St. Mary's University School of Law in San Antonio when we talked in 2017, possesses a younger generation's view of the ranch not unlike that of older members of the family:

I grew up here in the summers with a lot of life's first events happening here. I learned to drive here. I shot my first deer here. I proposed to my wife, Madison, on a bluff overlooking the creek about two hundred yards from this house. The ranch was our family's living room in a lot of ways, and the creek was a central part of that. There were many birthdays spent swimming down at the creek. A lot of campouts with friends that continued into college. I worked with the ranch staff building trails. All of it instilled in me a love for the outdoors and an appreciation for what our family has done with this property and a very careful understanding of what a special place this is.

The role Marshall will play in the ranch's future is uncertain, but he showed a firm grasp of the importance of planning land protection across generations when he spoke at a "Generations on the Land Summit" conference in Austin presented by the Texas Agricultural Land Trust. He outlined for attendees the progression of his family's care of their lands through nearly eighty years.

After purchasing the Shield Ranch, more remote properties were added: The Camp Wood Ranch, seventy-four hundred acres in Real County west of San Antonio, was purchased in 1945. In Big Bend's Jeff Davis County, the twenty-three thousand–acre Cherry Canyon Ranch was bought in 1950. Part of the Camp Wood Ranch has been under a conservation easement since 2012 to protect habitat for the endangered black-capped vireo. Wildlife conservation plans are in place at the Cherry Canyon Ranch. Day-to-day oversight of all three properties is the job of land steward Blake Murden, who earned a doctorate in wildlife management from Texas A&M University.

Marshall spoke at the conference about the decision to put 95 percent of the Shield Ranch under conservation easements by The Nature Conservancy and the City of Austin. It was a lengthy process engineered largely by his uncle Bob with key decisions by his mother, Vera, and grandmother Patricia. Balancing family and public interests in the ranch continues to be a challenging but rewarding experience, he said. A key, he noted, is getting honest views of future management of the property from the family's next generation. Vera has two sons and two daughters, and Bob has two daughters, all young adults.

A new master plan for the ranch was completed in 2017 to update the original one drawn up thirty years ago. "We shared what we love about the ranch and what it is that we want to see from the ranch long term. We pressed through that process and diverse expectations to find common ground with a renewed commitment and flexibility," Marshall told the conference attendees.

The conservation easements and their land-protection requirements are permanent, but the ranch goes well beyond that. Summer camp programs on the ranch have served hundreds of children and young adults. The ranch is a research laboratory for university studies of plant and animal life, with 450 plant species and 200 bird species identified on the land. A checklist for guests is available to mark off birds they've spotted, including permanent and seasonal resident birds, migrants, and visitors. Miles of maintained trails provide access to the land with minimal disruption. A historic dry goods/postal store and a settler's log cabin have been restored. A low-impact cow-calf operation of 100 to 120 head is spread across the ranch.

The original master plan completed in 1987 largely was an assessment of the ranch's geology, hydrology, flora, and fauna and a recognition of the far-reaching water-quality role played by the ranch's 6.3 miles of Barton Creek and the flow of its tributaries and springs. In a beautiful conceptual analogy, the plan described the Shield Ranch as a big ceramic bowl with hills along its rim. Barton Creek runs like a crack across its bottom, and Rocky Creek and Long Branch are smaller cracks down the sides. Water spills down the hills and into the creeks and eventually reaches the recharge zone of the Edwards Aquifer downstream.

The plan, which also was an analysis of pressures on the ranch thirty years ago, reads as if it could be describing 2017:

> Austin and the Hill Country to her west suffer the perils of popularity wherein that popularity is juxtaposed to an environment that is easily altered. The beauty and drama of these abrupt hills attract an admiring population: thus the paradox of how to at once preserve the land and enjoy it. As highways, utility systems, houses, offices and shopping centers creep westward, the concept of sensitive planning is put to the test.

> Political issues such as Austin's growing extraterritorial jurisdiction (ETJ) and the resulting impact of increased regulations and ordinances, the overlay of state highway interests . . . , the notorious issues surrounding wastewater disposal and potable water rights, and the incorporation and expansion of the community of Bee Cave—all these and more combine to make the region a complex of dynamic issues to monitor.

Not long after that first master plan was completed, Bob invited representatives of The Nature Conservancy office in San Antonio to visit the ranch.

Six miles of Barton Creek flow across sixty-eight hundred acres of conservation land.

Jeff Weigel and Helen Ballew toured the property and left brochures touting the values of conservation easements. The enabling legislation for such easements had only recently been passed by the Texas legislature, although they were in use in other states for years.

Ten years of family discussions and implementation of land improvements in the master plan passed before the Ayreses signed the easement documents at the old ranch house. At the same round table where they made that beneficent commitment, I ask what led to their final decision. Growing up in San Antonio, Bob had watched friends' ranches close to town get swallowed up by developers. "I wanted an alternate future for our ranch than that. Conservation easements were a tool we learned about that would enable us to own the property and keep some of its traditional uses. We could even retain some development rights for things we might want to do in the future but also permanently restrict the kind of development we didn't want to see, such as subdivisions and strip malls."

Twenty years ago, the prevailing Texas landowners' view was that such easements were a kind of government takeover plot. That was never the family's view, Bob says. "From the beginning, we had been interested in partnerships. If the goal was to protect the ranch and another entity was willing to hold the easement, then that was an assessment that the land was of conservation value and in the public interest to do so." Still, it was a big step for the family to encumber the land forever with the easements. That's like a marriage without the possibility of divorce. The deal also was a challenge in a landowning family where the property is held in an undivided interest. "We had to figure it out together or go to court. Those were the two options," Bob says. The 5 percent of the Shield Ranch not covered by the easements is valuable acreage fronting Hamilton Pool Road and Crumley Ranch Road near the ranch's back gate. Bob says nothing currently is planned for the land, but it is an asset that the family wants to retain and control.

What the conservation easements accomplished, in effect, was to extend the SOS Ordinance approved by Austin voters in 1992 across the ranch, even though much of the land is outside the city's extraterritorial jurisdiction. "That was a significant watershed restriction that did a lot for water quality upstream. For a while on the green spaces map there was just the Wilderness Park above the greenbelt, The Nature Conservancy's Barton Creek Habitat Preserve, and us, but now there are more and more tracts under easements," Bob notes.

Easements on the Shield Ranch and elsewhere in the Barton Creek watershed appear to have made a difference over the past decade with fewer algae blooms and other signs of fouled water reported. Reintroduction of native grasses, rotational grazing, and low cattle stocking rates are among the reasons. "Grasses on the ranch are improving and, in turn, improving Barton Creek's water quality and quantity. We're offsetting what is happening downstream with so much development in Bee Cave and elsewhere," Bob tells me. It was a major honor, but no surprise, that the Shield Ranch was chosen by the Texas Parks & Wildlife Department in 2000 for its annual statewide Lone Star Land Steward Award. The family's commitment to effective land-management practices has been recognized and praised by many state conservation groups.

After working throughout 2017 with national and local experts in landscape design, ecological restoration, and water resources, the eleven members of the family completed a new master plan for the ranch. Christy Muse, director of external relations for the ranch, summarized the agreed guiding vision: "The plan will unveil programs and experiences that will allow the uniqueness of the ranch to be more broadly shared with the larger community. The goal is to educate, inspire, and transform people."

Among the new outreaches will be creation of a small retreat center in a quiet, remote part of the ranch to accommodate overnight guests and day visitors. Retreats might bring in spiritual and nonprofit groups, conservation organizations, artists and writers, or corporate gatherings. More permanent structures will be built for the El Ranchito nature immersion summer program for youths whose families otherwise could not afford a camp. That will allow additional year-round programming and access to groups for campouts, retreats, hikes, and other events. A new system of trails in Chalk Knob Hollow will show off the natural beauty of this unaltered small tributary to Barton Creek. Another evolving plan is for research in wildlife habitat and biodiversity.

Patricia, Bob, and Vera live in Austin, and none of their offspring have moved to the ranch. Like her son Marshall, Vera says that might be something for her to consider in the future. Family residences could be built under the easement allowances. The rambling old ranch house and a newer adjacent guesthouse are used primarily for family events such as meetings, weddings, and weekend visits—and for big Thanksgiving gatherings for the past twenty years.

Vera now runs the family's Shield-Ayres Foundation, a charitable organization that since the 1970s has been helping the disadvantaged in need of health and other human services. More than $22 million over the years has funded local, state, and national nonprofit organizations working on clean-water accessibility, housing issues, early childhood and environmental education, and arts programs. The foundation also has assisted in international disaster relief efforts. A separate Shield Ranch Foundation operates the El Ranchito conservation camps for youths.

In the 1970s, Bob and Vera accompanied their father, Robert M. Ayres Jr., to Honduras and Guatemala as volunteers after natural disasters there. "That gave us a larger view of the world and our responsibilities," Vera says. Bob earned a master's degree from Virginia Theological Seminary but not necessarily for an Episcopal ministry. The family's foundations have given him other ways to help people.

The wealth that allows the family to do so much stems from 1933, when Fred W. Shield started an oil leasing company in San Antonio and became a successful independent oil and gas explorer and producer. The daughter of Fred and Vera Shield, Patricia Anne Shield, married Robert Moss Ayres Jr. in 1955. (The Ayreses were prominent in San Antonio during the early twentieth century when architects Atlee B. Ayres and his son Robert M. Ayres designed private and public buildings around the state.) Robert Jr.'s success as an investment banker allowed the couple to create the Shield-Ayres Foundation, which grew significantly through a bequest from Fred Shield's estate after his death in 1987.

El Ranchito was created in 2007 as a nature-immersion summer camp for at-risk youths. Partners who help select the attendees are El Buen Samaritano Episcopal Mission in Austin and the Westcave Outdoor Learning Center at a preserve on the Pedernales River. El Ranchito encompasses the Nature Discovery Camp (grades 4–9), Conservation Corps (grades 10–12), and Gulf Coast Expedition (ages 18–22), a headwaters-to-tidewaters learning and service journey for college students on the Texas coast.

Eager to sample a camp session in 2017, I meet Bob on the edge of a meadow as the boys and girls emerge from their tents for morning stretch routines and breakfast. Twenty preteens form a circle in the meadow, shaking out overnight kinks and acting out "Banana Song" silliness when the ranch's land steward, Blake Murden, trots up to the group on his horse Otis. It is a wow moment for the kids after their second night of camp. Blake tells the wide-eyed youths from Austin's inner city that he is on his way to rounding up cattle and needs help branding them. It is a bit of a fib but part of the program's history role-playing. The story line for the morning: It is the 1870s, and three families will hike separately to different locations for branding practice, toy making, and storytelling. The

El Ranchito summer camp brings dozens of at-risk youths to the ranch.

kids divide into groups and choose family names. Meet the Joneses, the Dreamers, and the Nachitos.

During breakfast, I talk to a couple of the young counselors. Ruben Coupal, eighteen, first came to the El Ranchito camp when he was in fourth grade. He's been here every year since. This summer he's a counselor for the first time. "I want to do something in the environmental sciences," he tells me. "But first I'd like to join AmeriCorps, maybe in Idaho. Or maybe I'll go into the Peace Corps." He sees choices, lots of them, now that he has stayed in school and learned about the larger world beyond what usually is seen by kids from low-income families. The camp is open to youths whose families qualify for the federal free-lunch program.

Another first-year counselor is Nancy Zepeda. The self-assured twenty-one-year-old describes herself as Guatemala born and Austin raised. She has no doubt at this point about her future direction. "I want to be a midwife. I'm going to a school for that in Hawaii this fall. Ever since I experienced my first home birth not long ago, that's my goal. It was such a beautiful sight with this mother, standing up, and delivering a child into a midwife's hands at her home. That's what I want to learn how to do."

After breakfast, the campers and counselors head off to their three history-lesson stations. At the branding stop, Paul Vickery is wielding several hot irons in a small fire. Vickery is on loan from the Westcave Preserve, where he is education director. No cattle are at the stop, but the kids don't seem to care as they line up to pick out a brand and get it burned onto a square piece of leather they can keep. Sophia proudly shows me the "S" brand she picks out as a symbol of her name. Bob offers the boys and girls his insight into what it is like when a cow is branded: "The smell of its hair burning is really strong."

Knee-high wire baskets filled with stones mark trails between the history stations. Along the Barton Creek tributary of Rocky Creek, a precarious trail at the top of a high bluff follows an ancient barbed-wire fence line. Some of the oldest cedar posts are left in place so the kids can see how fencing once was built. Eleven miles of trails traverse the ranch.

At the next stop, two women in bonnets and long dresses demonstrate the toys available to rural families in the 1870s. The kids like trying out a cup-and-ball game that tests their ability to swing a small ball tied to a long wood handle into a cup at the other end of the handle. The record, the pioneer women tell them, is 232 times in a row by a Toronto man. The kids groan as they attempt just one landing. The women show them corn-husk dolls, rag dolls without stitching, and wood-spoon dolls with painted faces. "The pioneer families out here were the ultimate recyclers, who used old clothes and old pieces of wood for their toys," the youths are told.

As the El Ranchito kids complete their history rounds, Bob and I move on to see the old store on the ranch where nearly a century ago area families bought supplies and mailed letters. The long and sturdy stone building recently underwent "pointing" renewal to replace deteriorated mortar between the stone blocks. El Ranchito's older Conservation Corps campers did the work on what is called the Walburg Store, built in the 1870s by an immigrant proprietor from Prussia. Bob says the store operated into the 1930s until a series of droughts curtailed area farming and ranching. "My grandfather kept feed and other things here after he bought the property in 1938," Bob says. "What we didn't realize until recent years is that a stone wall was built in a large rectangle around the store. Most of it is long gone, but with the help of geomapping we could see where it had stood. It was another aha moment for me out here."

Next, we head for the 1870s log cabin that sits above a bend of Rocky Creek, a reliable, spring-fed feeder of Barton Creek. To get there, we walk between the ruts worn in the limestone by bygone wagons. Attention to preserving such details of history is a hallmark of Bob's interest in the land. The cabin was restored in 1991 with a careful rebuilding of the crumbling chimney and a new cypress-shake roof to match the original. A short distance down Rocky Creek from the cabin, a bald cypress tree towers over the oaks, elms, and pecans. The tree was planted next to a spring decades ago by the mother of Fred Haas, who owned the ranch before Bob's grandfather. "We had a supper here when the restoration was finished, and Mr. Haas, who was in his nineties then, came

The story of the Shield Ranch's old store is one Bob Ayres relishes telling.

with bright red suspenders and a lot of tales to tell. Some probably were true," Bob says with a laugh at the memory. He says an old woman was living in the cabin on a twenty-five-acre inholding when his grandfather purchased the ranch. She later sold the parcel to Bob's grandfather. "It's been fun all these years learning more and more about the ranch and its history in the area."

I ask about endangered birds on the Shield Ranch. One breeding pair of black-capped vireos was here, but Bob says there's no recurring population now. "Over time, we have seen golden-cheeked warblers spreading out on the ranch as older cedars get to keep growing by managing that habitat." We stop at a large pecan tree canopy in the middle of a field where five trunks grow almost like it is one tree. Bob says the field likely was plowed decades ago and the pecan tree was cut down. Then it sprouted anew and grew into five trunks. The resiliency-of-nature lesson is one of many he enjoys telling visitors to the ranch. He talks about controlled burns to thin the cedars and working with Trinity University students on ways to curtail King Ranch bluestem, an invasive grass species. Seasonal hunting keeps the deer population in check. Six old windmills on the ranch have been replaced with solar-powered motors because Bob says it is tough these days to find someone to repair windmills.

Water-quality samples from Barton Creek are analyzed by city Watershed Protection Department biologists who visit the ranch regularly. The results have been good thus far, but Bob says he is waiting to see what effects will come from nearby developments. The Rocky Creek subdivision, which encompasses a fork of the tributary that flows into the Shield Ranch and joins Barton Creek there, is nearing completion. Another, bigger subdivision called Provence began clearing land around Little Barton Creek in 2018 on Hamilton Pool Road close to the ranch's main entrance.

When the Rocky Creek subdivision is built out, it will have 395 homes on 468 acres stretching from Hamilton Pool Road to Crumley Ranch Road. The development, where homes average $613,000, could be anywhere in suburbia with houses jammed backyard to backyard. They are clustered so close together because about three hundred acres in the Rocky Creek riparian areas were left for green space and irrigation areas for the on-site wastewater treatment facility. Extensive trails along and above the creek provide the quiet country feel missing from the residential streets. But the effluent pipes and spraying spigots poke up beside the trails as reminders of the subdivision's infrastructure.

Bob and a small group of nearby landowners called Hamilton Pool Road Matters contested the wastewater permits for both the Provence and Rocky Creek developments with the Texas Commission on Environmental Quality. Rocky Creek's developer and the landowners mutually funded an irrigation study by Texas A&M University scientists. As a result, the subdivision now irrigates treated wastewater onto native vegetation rather than exotic grasses. "We got other concessions from Rocky Creek over such issues as extra safeguards at the treatment facility," Bob says of the steps that are legally binding by the settlement agreement. "We haven't seen water-quality degradation from there yet."

A mediated permit settlement was reached with the Provence developer, Jim Meredith, who plans 664 homes on the 460 acres he bought. Initially, he had sought water service for more than 1,600 lots and roadside commercial buildings on 910 acres that included another landowners' acreage to the north. But the West Travis County Public Utility Agency denied that request. Neighbors in the Hamilton Pool Road Matters group objected to the development for four years, citing pollution risks to the creek, the strain on water supplies, and the increased traffic it would bring to the narrow, winding Hamilton Pool Road. Meredith says he wants the road improved, too, and plans to pay for a traffic light at the entrance to Provence. The size and density of Provence still amount to what the Shield Ranch's Christy Muse describes as "a game changer for the area" that could encourage more large developments.

It's not just housing developments that threaten the Barton Creek watershed. Vera says one reason for choosing the conservation easements was the Outer Loop highway proposal first floated in the late 1980s. Dubbed State Highway 45, the expressway would have skirted the ranch's east side to connect US 290 on the south to Ranch Road 620 into Lakeway and across the Colorado River to communities in northern Travis County. Development no doubt would have followed along the route. "That road was the impetus for us getting engaged in the master planning effort. We had a clear understanding then that the road didn't mesh with our plans," she says.

The state's economic recession of the late 1980s and early 1990s put the loop plan into dormancy, but versions of it still rear up occasionally. The latest was in 2014 when the City of Lakeway proposed a feasibility study of a six-lane highway route through southwestern Travis County. Bob was among those who lobbied against the idea, and it was withdrawn the following year. The easements on the Shield Ranch do not preclude condemnation for roads and utilities.

What could become an Outer Loop link, Texas 45 SW, now is being built across south Austin to connect MoPac and FM 1826 with roads in Buda near Interstate 35. In 2017, the Save Our Springs Alliance fought in federal court without success to stop the project because it is plowing through endangered bird habitat and laying pavement across the recharge zone of the Edwards Aquifer. In the Barton Creek watershed to the north, another controversial road plan would pave the 3.5-mile private Reimers-Peacock Road and open up land to developers with a new connection between Texas 71 west of Bee Cave and Hamilton Pool Road. Travis County commissioners declined to put the project in a 2017 bonds package, but no one thinks the idea is dead. The roads-first pressure to get access to acreage not far from the Shield Ranch appears relentless.

The Ayreses and Bowens, with their carefully considered visions of the future, remain resolved to craft a conservation-land showcase unlike any other in the region. They want to invite more people onto the ranch to learn from and see the results of years of ecological work. They want to introduce the wonders of nature to more youths. They want to create a retreat center where quiet and a contemplative spirit reign. I have no doubt they'll accomplish it all. The master-plan process in the 1980s drew the family together and led them to conservation easements. The new master plan promises a wider sharing of the ranch's natural bounties.

Vera Bowen says the long discussions and planning to ensure the inviolability of the Shield Ranch produced an important side benefit: "For me personally, the process gave us a common project to work out relationship issues. We learned to communicate effectively and come to a commitment. We've always been loyal to one another, but the ranch decision helped us get closer to one another."

Following photos and interviews with family members, Alberto and I climb into Bob's SUV with Patricia and Vera to see one of the family's swimming holes on Barton Creek below an old concrete low-water crossing. The water is clear and flowing but not very high. It's easy to see the white limestone creek bed beneath the surface under a clear blue sky. The summer has been a dry one, but Vera tells us what it was like many times at this spot when her family was growing up. "I'd drop my kids in tubes into the water just downstream of here. See how the creek narrows and turns between those cliffs? It can be a very fast chute. Schlitterbahn had nothing on us then."

We return to the ranch in the fall to take stock of the creek again. The six miles of water winding

Four generations on the ranch have splashed in the creek's Blue Hole.

through here in the middle of Barton Creek's journey into Austin is a stunning portrait of natural beauty. Shades of green that framed the banks all summer give way to leaves of gold and rust. The water flows with more urgency, spilling over ledges in frothy churns. Tall bluffs of rock strata, with faces of white in places and black in others, line the far side of the creek, then disappear entirely. For eons, the creek has carved through this land of dozens of hills and valleys. It alternately shoved against stone and gently spread out over low grasslands, depending on the strength and frequency of rains. Springs and tributaries contributed to the creek flow in shifting volumes.

We walk to the Blue Hole where a young Patricia Shield jumped off boulders and picnicked with her parents and friends decades ago. The water is wider in this spot near the ranch's most distant gravel road crossing. The creek's deep blue color hides its depth, while keeper-length fish glide in formation close to the surface. I try to hear the bygone echoes of laughter and splashing as dusk sneaks in. Above the opposite creek bank, on the bare top branches of an old tree, four turkeys settle in for the night. I wonder if they can see the lights turning on in new hilltop developments nearby. This protected and loved land feels a million miles removed.

6 WILD GREENBELT

Pleasures, Dangers, and Challenges in Canyons above Barton Springs

Barton Creek displays many different moods as it alternately tumbles over rocks and gently flows across flats for more than seven miles through Austin's public but still wild greenbelt. Upstream from Barton Springs Pool in Zilker Park, the greenbelt twists with the creek to the southwest roughly parallel to MoPac Boulevard. Then it turns to the northwest and follows Loop 360. Houses, apartments, office buildings, and the city's biggest shopping mall loom above.

Often the creek is thirsty for water in the late summer when nothing falls from the sky for weeks. Much of the lower greenbelt then looks like a rocky, white desert of boulders and limestone expanses and deep cracks where the water has disappeared into the aquifer. The popular swimming spots of Campbell's Hole and Gus Fruh Pool keep some still water. Upstream waterfalls flow with meager volumes thanks to several nearby springs. Swimmable sections usually can be found below the falls.

Even on the hottest, driest days, hikers and bikers and sunbathers visit the greenbelt. The canyons and dense woodlands shade parts of the creek bed and the trails with a few degrees of coolness. It's decidedly more comfortable down here than on the streets

Trails wind through seven miles of the Barton Creek Greenbelt and Wilderness Park.

above. When rains come and Barton Creek fills with fresh water—no matter the season—the greenbelt can be as crowded as Zilker Park. People flock to the falls and swimming holes. Many bring their dogs and their beverages. Others walk slowly beside the creek just to soak in views of the beauty of it all—clear water flowing and swirling over and around rocks of every shape, size, and hue. Calm, deep sections of water reflect the trees, bushes, and grasses along the banks.

The Barton Creek Greenbelt and the upstream Barton Creek Wilderness Park—most people collectively call them the city's greenbelt—offer an urban oasis without picnic tables or ball fields. Trail markers point the way and distances between markers. Several trailhead kiosks with maps stand near access parking areas. Still, it is easy to get lost on the many paths worn off the main trails. On weekdays when summer is over and school and college classes have resumed, quiet is the dominant feature of the greenbelt. Birds and breezes and the occasional coyote, fox, or raccoon make some noise, but not enough to break the solitude.

Everything changes when hard, flooding rains fill the creek over a day or two. The greenbelt literally roars then. The canyon hillsides keep the water from spreading out and slowing down. The creek's steep elevation drop on its journey through the greenbelt moves the water at breakneck speed. When the creek is a torrent, it attracts sightseers, skilled kayakers, and risk-taking swimmers and tubers. It can kill. It did just that in late May and early June 2016, claiming three lives.

On June 6, Barton Springs Pool lifeguard Ceazar Kainz took advantage of a Monday off work with lots of water flowing down Barton Creek. He headed with friends to Sculpture Falls, a popular swimming and gathering spot near the upstream end of the greenbelt. Kainz, twenty-four, lived in Cedar Park and had worked nights for three years at Rain on 4th, a downtown Austin nightclub. Parking in a neighborhood near a trailhead off Loop 360, the group walked down a steep, eroded limestone hillside named the Hill of Life. He and his friends swam for a short while near the falls, where water buried boulders and ledges. The group decided to get out because the current was too swift, but Ceazar said he wanted to stay a bit longer and would catch up with them. That was the last they saw him. His body was found the next day in debris downstream.

Cassidy Stillwell, a friend of Ceazar and a fellow lifeguard at the pool, was not with Ceazar's group that day, but the pain of loss was evident when I talked to him nearly a year later. "A lot of us were pretty angry with him after he died. He shouldn't have been by himself in a flood. He was one of the strongest swimmers here. It was a sobering time for all the lifeguards," he says as we stand outside the guards' room at Barton Springs Pool. The pool staff planted a dogwood tree on the south lawn in honor of their friend. "Ceazar was one of those people who working with him was always a pleasure. He was so positive, a really beautiful soul."

A chilling note is that Ceazar, just a week before his death, was among the lifeguards who gathered at the upstream end of the pool as the body of thirty-four-year-old Leah Durrett was pulled from the creek bypass grate. Heavy rains had made the creek's current dangerous then, but she had joined friends tubing on May 30, beginning at Twin Falls five miles upstream of where her body was discovered.

On June 11, five days after Ceazar's death, Hansel Rene Hernandez-Garay went missing while swimming in a stretch of the creek near Loop 360. The fifteen-year-old Houston boy's body was found later that day. Three weeks later, on the Fourth of July, another death occurred on the greenbelt when twenty-year-old Thomas White, a student at Southwestern University in Georgetown, fell down a fifty-foot cliff while hiking. He and three friends were negotiating a narrow trail above a cliff known as Whiteface or Land Bridge when he slipped. White was a soccer player at Southwestern.

Deaths and injuries from falls on rugged trails high in the greenbelt are not uncommon. On April 1, 2017, a thirty-one-year-old man fell fifty to one hundred feet from a cliff near the 3500 block of South Lamar Boulevard. The death of Mark Creasy, an Austin software developer and martial arts practitioner, was where Barton Creek loops far below popular restaurants and apartments. Park rangers say the greenbelt is deceptive because hikers can easily go within minutes from creek-level, well-worn trails to wilder, unmarked paths at higher elevations. The small staff of rangers patrol the main trails on foot, but they can cover only a fraction of the greenbelt's eighteen hundred acres. They advise people to wear sturdy hiking shoes, carry a first-aid kit, and bring a map of the trails.

Safety entering the creek during high-water periods takes a bit of CFS knowledge. Cubic feet per second is the standard measurement of the rate at which water flows by volume in a river or creek. One CFS translates into a flow of roughly 450 gallons a minute. The Austin Fire Department, which responds to swift-water emergencies on the creek, uses CFS flow rates in deciding when to declare the creek unsafe and closed for recreation. The city's Waterway Restriction Guide assists officials in determining when waterway closures are appropriate. The guide, last revised in 2014, was being reviewed in late 2017. According to the guide, up to 350 CFS is considered a recreational flow safe for swimming, tubing, kayaks, canoes, and other watercraft. The range 350–750 CFS is considered a challenging flow, with swimming and tubing not recommended. Hard-shell kayaks and the wearing of helmets and life jackets are recommended for 750–1,500 CFS, considered a dangerous flow.

At a flow rate of more than 1,500 CFS, or when debris in and along the water is a safety issue, the fire department will announce that Barton Creek in the greenbelt is closed to everyone. The department also could close the creek at a lower flow rate if heavy rainfall is happening upstream or is predicted in the area. Closure signs are posted and gates are locked at access points, but those measures are easily ignored or circumvented. On the May day in 2016 when Leah Durrett drowned, the flow reached 850 CFS. Later that summer on August 16 and 17 the creek was flowing at 2,250 CFS, and the fire department made a closure announcement. The fire department makes announcements of creek closings on news and social media. There are no warnings issued when the flow is below 1,500 CFS for fear that inexperienced people will be attracted by the news of swift water and attempt to float or paddle the creek.

Where to check the CFS? The current and recent flow rates for four sites on Barton Creek (at the upper dam above Barton Springs Pool and at the crossings of Loop 360, Lost Creek Boulevard, and Texas 71) are posted on US Geological Survey (USGS) websites. Search for USGS Barton Creek to see the current conditions for each site on separate links. A new website developed by a University of Texas student in 2018 uses USGS data to post approximate water depth and flow figures at popular swimming sites on the Barton Creek greenbelt only. There is not a USGS measuring station at each site to draw from, but the map and information at www.greenbeltnow.com is easy to read as a basic guide to daily conditions.

When floods threaten, the National Weather Service will issue advisories based on expected flood-stage levels of waterways. For Barton Creek, a major flood-stage level is a crest of 12 feet. The record measurement in May 1929 was a crest of 26 feet. The second-highest crest was in October 2015 at 19.1 feet. At that record 26 feet, USGS calculates the flow would have been 44,400 CFS. The flow of Arizona's Colorado River through the Grand Canyon in the commercial rafting season averages about a third that at 12,000 to 15,000 CFS.

I wish I had paid attention to what's safe when in the early 1990s I took two small rafts downstream with my young son, a coworker, and his young daughter. We left from the creek crossing at Lost Creek Boulevard and were soon swept into an uncomfortably fast current. More than once we slammed into islands of small rocks and trees in the middle of the creek. We spilled from the rafts a couple of times in rapids but hung onto them with ropes. It was an exhausting trip that scared us and made me respect the power of Barton Creek.

My fonder memories are like those of most visitors to the greenbelt. Cool, deep swimming holes with rope swings. Boulders to jump from. Trails that lead beneath dripping rock overhangs covered with ferns. Afternoons lounging atop gentle waterfalls. Quiet walks alone on the long trails beside the creek. It is an incredibly beautiful slice of nature in the middle of Austin's urban bustle.

Although most people refer to the entire seven-mile wooded stretch of Barton Creek from the pool to Lost Creek subdivision as the greenbelt, Ted Siff is always going to distinguish the newer Wilderness Park end from the older Barton Creek Greenbelt start. He was instrumental in greatly expanding the narrow city greenbelt, which officially opened in 1985 after several years of land purchases in the face of development encroaching on the area. The Wilderness Park added a much wider and wilder treasure of protected land.

In the 1950s, talk began about how to create a natural park in the canyons upstream of Barton Springs Pool. City parks director Beverly Sheffield suggested building a two-lane vehicle parkway along the creek. It would be modeled after the Blue Ridge Parkway built in the 1930s in Virginia and North Carolina. The idea didn't get far. A petition drive in 1970 left out the cars. A group called Citizens for a Barton Creek Park proposed a thirteen-mile hiking extension of Zilker Park to the Texas 71 highway. The group's open letter to the City Council expressed how valuable the area was to the city's identity:

> There are not—there cannot be—very many cities of the size of Austin around the world that are blessed with such an extraordinary enclave of wilderness so close to the heart of downtown. A free-flowing stream with rapids, with pools that reflect precipitous bluffs, a marvel of variety in colors, textures and shapes, a place to see flowers rarely seen in a city, to hear bird songs rarely heard by city dwellers—these are assets of inestimable value to the residents of Austin.

The park proposal stalled, however, when it faced the high costs of land along the creek. Finally, city voters approved a bond issue in 1975. But purchase negotiations were tough, and all the money was not spent for ten years, as land prices continued to escalate. In 1985, the greenbelt park officially opened as a narrow strip of land and creek reaching only to MoPac Boulevard. Seven more years passed until August 8, 1992, when voters approved $20 million in bonds to create the Wilderness Park of about 1,050 acres. The greenbelt downstream comprises about 800 acres. The vote was on the same ballot with Austin's SOS Ordinance and $22 million in bonds for the Balcones Canyonlands Conservation Plan. All three measures passed, putting a giant stamp of approval on the environmental movement that coalesced after the 1990 all-night City Council development hearing dubbed the Barton Springs Uprising.

The methodical march to create the Wilderness Park was led by Citizens for Open Space and the Save Barton Creek Association. Ted Siff was president of the citizens group formed in early 1991. The group soon commissioned a public opinion survey, which showed overwhelming voter support for the acquisition of open-space land to protect water quality. The bond proposition in 1992 targeted several parcels of land for the Wilderness Park, with the Gaines tract on the south side of the creek accounting for about 750 of the 1,050 acres. The properties were the last remaining undeveloped areas of the Barton Creek watershed in the recharge zone of the Edwards Aquifer.

"The idea was to advocate for what land shouldn't be developed. It was an alternative to the raping and pillaging of the land that was occurring through the private sector. There weren't significant environment

Sculpture Falls graces the greenbelt's Wilderness Park.

regulations at the time," Ted recalls. He and city activist Beverly Griffith "took people on dozens of tours to show them the land. We trespassed. It was all privately owned. Some of it on the Loop 360 side had been bought by speculative developers." Environmentalists Helen Ballew and George Cofer also helped shape the bond campaign. "Our group got technical help from the National Park Service's river trails assistance program that showed this land was the most important land to save Barton Springs," says Ted. "If development happened on this land, which was the heart of the recharge zone, pollution could percolate down to the aquifer and pollute Barton Springs faster and more substantially than anything that might happen upstream. We made the argument that if anything needed to be not developed, it was this land. We won that argument."

I ask Ted if the bonds vote surprised him, and he says he never took the outcome for granted. "That $20 million is the equivalent of $200 million today, so it was a huge investment and nothing like it had been approved before. Most bond issues for parkland then were for $3 million or $4 million. Plus, the $22 million for the Balcones Canyonlands was on the same ballot and that won by a similar margin."

The two propositions created the core landholdings of the Balcones plan, which encompassed the Wilderness Park and many noncontiguous tracts stretching north to Lake Travis. It took nearly twenty more years for the city, county, and federal government to buy land in the plan. Some bond votes failed. Of the 125,000 acres envisioned in the plan, more than 31,000 acres wound up protected by the local governments and 27,500 in the Balcones Canyonlands

National Wildlife Refuge northwest of Austin. The Wilderness Park includes habitat for the endangered golden-cheeked warbler and the black-capped vireo. But the park's open-access trails and public creek use distinguish it from the other, mostly closed lands in the Balcones Canyonlands network. The federal refuge includes about 3,000 acres open to the public.

The Wilderness Park acquisitions happened more quickly than many of the other Balcones purchases because so much of the acreage was held by one owner, the Gaines Ranch family. The Gaines deal came first, with the family selling their property along Barton Creek to the city but keeping a smaller, less environmentally sensitive tract along MoPac that they later sold to a developer. The eight other parcels were purchased over the next ten years.

What is Ted's favorite part of the Wilderness Park? "Probably Sculpture Falls, but there are lots of special places that are just total wilderness. I hike a lot and have hiked the park numerable times. Yet every time I go there I have a special experience." He says the Hill of Life, an eroded, steep series of natural limestone steps leading to Sculpture Falls, has turned out more popular than expected. "It's amazing how much more athletic people are now than they were twenty-five years ago when we first opened that up."

Ted now is board president of the Shoal Creek Conservancy, which is working to improve the flood-prone eleven-mile creek along the original west side of downtown Austin. He is eager to make Shoal Creek an urban greenbelt just steps from businesses and high-rises, extending the current 3.25-mile trail north to the creek's headwaters near US 183. It won't require the purchase of huge amounts of acreage, so I'm confident Ted and the conservancy's supporters will bring the project to fruition in the next several years.

The Wilderness Park's stars are Twin Falls just west of MoPac and Sculpture Falls upstream off Loop 360. They are the most popular gathering spots on the creek for people who don't mind a hike to where they can sit and swim amid the splashing waters. The quickest way to Twin Falls is to park on the MoPac turnaround road just west of Loop 360 and take a half-mile trail down to the creek. The youthful crowds that favor Twin Falls fill that parking area on sunny days. In dry periods, the falls can be far more exposed rock than cascading water. Sculpture Falls, where the water depth is more dependable, is a mile and a half upstream of Twin Falls. Most people access it from streetside parking on Camp Craft Road in a neighborhood off Loop 360. The Hill of Life is the tough beginning section at the top of the trailhead, while the remainder is a flat trail downstream along the creek. While the main trail through the Wilderness Park hugs the north side of Barton Creek and can be hiked with relative ease (beware muddy sections after rains and poison ivy nearly year-round), other trails in the park can be difficult. Mountain bikers love them, pedaling up the hillsides to flat areas networked by more trails.

I enjoy hiking on the less traveled trails. Only once did I have a negative experience, taking a trail upstream of Sculpture Falls. Here the narrow path leads over craggy terrain, up against cliffs, and across soggy streams that run down to the creek. A friend and I were glad we wore sturdy hiking boots. What surprised us was that our passage into the Lost Creek subdivision took us behind its aging sewage treatment plant. I knew the plant was somewhere in this area not far from the Lost Creek Boulevard bridge that goes over the creek to the subdivision's golf course. But I didn't expect the foul stench coming from the plant that day. Nor did I know the plant was just a few yards up from the bank of Barton Creek.

We hurried along the narrow footpath on the backside of the plant to get upwind of the smell and into the open air of the trail's end at the bridge. This was in August 2016. Days later I read and saw news coverage of sewage leaks at the plant. Forty nearby residents filed a complaint with the Texas Commission on Environmental Quality after a sewage tank at the

Looming over the creek is Barton Hills, a neighborhood dating to the 1940s.

plant leaked at least twice that month. They worried that if the tank leaked again, the sewage could make its way into Barton Creek. The City of Austin took over maintenance of the plant in 2014 after decades of operation by the Lost Creek Municipal Utility District.

The problem turned out to be a plywood lid put on the equalization tank by the MUD. It was rotting away, and partially treated sewage was spilling from the top of the tank. City workers fixed the problem with a new metal lid and replaced a failed sensor that should have alerted them to the high level of sewage in the tank. Nothing made its way into Barton Creek, they said. Today, a sizable sewage treatment plant like this would not be built so close to Barton Creek. But smaller "package" treatment plants are being built in new subdivisions beyond Austin's boundaries. Some are not far from tributaries that feed the creek.

In early 2018, I talked my way into the Lost Creek plant for a quick look. A worker there showed me the tank that overflowed and explained how new pumps had been put in to make sure the sewage would be contained if another problem occurred. "It's just old," he said. "These things need to be updated." The subdivision of Lost Creek was built in 1976 and expanded

WILD GREENBELT : **61**

over the years with more houses. It could have been greenbelt land instead. W. H. Bullard, who lived on twenty-five hundred acres above the creek, offered to sell his land to the city in the 1960s. The asking price was $300 an acre. "It was an awful little bit of money. They said the city is not in the real estate business," Bullard recalled in a 1982 newspaper article. He sold the land in the early 1970s, and a developer's bulldozers began to roll in.

The greenbelt takes a near-circular loop between mile 2 and mile 4 that many people regard as its most picturesque segment. The Gus Fruh Pool trail access in Barton Hills leads down switchbacks to the creek and a swimming hole. A rope swing tied high up in a tree on the creek bank deposits energetic swimmers almost to the middle of the water. A rock wall a short distance upstream is popular with climbers. Downstream, hikers pass dramatic limestone cliffs. The woods are thick between the creek's looping sides, and it is easy to get lost on trails worn through the brush and trees off the main marked route. It is hard to believe that busy South Lamar Boulevard with restaurants and shops is just over the horizon of the bluffs. The far end of this creek circle passes under the Loop 360 and MoPac cloverleaf, where another swimming hole and several rope swings draw visitors. A new view overhead from this spot is the bike and pedestrian pathway bridge that the city hopes will take some commuters off the roads.

Accessibility to this area of the greenbelt increased in 2015 with the opening of the first section of the Violet Crown Trail. Spearheaded by the Hill Country Conservancy, the trail is envisioned as a thirty-mile route leading south from Barton Creek through the Sunset Valley suburb and the Lady Bird Johnson Wildflower Center, and eventually to conservation lands in the Onion Creek watershed. The initial Violet Crown trailhead along US 290 in Sunset Valley provides a steep, switchback pathway through a mile and a half of thick woods and across several tributary streams down to Barton Creek.

At the bottom of the trail, hikers can choose to

A church group spends the day picking up trash as they hike and explore.

follow the creek upstream toward Twin Falls or downstream toward the Barton Hills loop. Either direction they are likely to find increasing numbers of people enjoying a break from the urban busyness above. Unfortunately, they also will find evidence of what some visitors to the greenbelt leave behind. Keeping the greenbelt clean is the job of a handful of workers for the Austin Parks and Recreation Department. The crew leader, a nearly twenty-year veteran of the department, is Mark Salinas. Mark has seen the results of more and more visitors to the greenbelt: Trash cans at trailhead accesses overflowing by the end of the day. Multicolored mutt mitts full of what dog owners pick up but then leave as tied-up plastic packets along the creek. Graffiti painted on boulders, on flat parts of the creek, and on cliff faces. Empty beer bottles and cans tossed near popular waterfall gathering spots.

It all depresses the native Austinite, who knows there are no easy answers with so many miles of heavily wooded canyons open to the public. Since he started working out of the maintenance facility at Zilker Park in 2000, Mark says he has seen the amount of graffiti scars on the greenbelt ebb and flow. When I talked to him in the summer of 2017, he said it was on the increase. "I don't get it. You're out in nature and you need to put your name on it? Even the mile-marker posts on the trail get marked."

He and his crew try to blast away the graffiti with pressurized water hoses, but it's tough when the creek water is insufficient or graffiti is high on a cliff without access to water. They are trying out a portable system, but the ten-gallon water tanks carried on four-wheelers don't last long. When he first started working the greenbelt, one or two fifty-five-gallon trash barrels at trailhead access points were enough. Now, he says in the peak summertime, ten barrels a day are not enough. I ask if trash cans could be put down on the creek, but he says then no one would bring anything up. It would be too difficult to remove the trash, and animals would get to it. "It's just the volume of people. We'll iron it out, but it's a moving target." Mutt mitts left down by the creek is another thing Mark says "I just don't get. They go to the trouble of picking it up but then leave the bags behind." Dogs also are a

Graffiti mars nature's beauty on the greenbelt and challenges city workers.

WILD GREENBELT : 63

problem when allowed to go off leash. Coyotes have mauled more than one of them, and several have suffered snakebites.

The Texas Conservation Corps and other volunteer youth groups help the city remove invasive plant species such as ligustrum trees that otherwise would take over the trails and creek banks. Litter patrols from other service groups sometimes simply show up on the greenbelt. Photographer Alberto Martinez and I went looking for city workers removing graffiti in July 2017 when we ran into one band of eager volunteers with trash bags. Thirteen youths ages seven to twelve were picking up litter and dog-waste packets as fast as they could walk along the creek near Campbell's Hole. They were part of the Urban Mission Outreach of Resurrection Episcopal Church in north Austin. The Reverend Billy Tweedie and the kids had taken a bus to Zilker Park for the day with the mission to clean up the creek. "It makes them aware of the environment and gets them thinking about how they will treat something like Barton Creek," Tweedie tells us.

Another kind of greenbelt patrol duty is no easy walk in the woods for the city's park rangers. They go out primarily on foot and contend with some very tough issues. Without peace officer powers, they can't arrest anyone, issue citations, or even ask for identification. The rangers' only legal option is to call the Austin Police Department if they see someone involved in lawbreaking. Yet they see evidence of that all the time—littering, unleashed dogs, underage drinking, public drunkenness, cooking fires, and destruction of public property (a.k.a. graffiti).

The rangers rarely call police, preferring education instead. They talk to greenbelt users one on one and to groups they encounter. In a friendly way, they explain the rules, dispense commonsense advice, and plead for help keeping the creek and the trails safe. Sandra Heath is education outreach superintendent on the rangers' staff of about twenty people (that includes twelve-hour shifts every day of the week and patrol duties in Zilker Park and a few other city parks).

She knows the greenbelt well from years of running on trails for exercise and the challenge.

"There are not that many places like this with so many trails and a beautiful stream running through the rolling hills," she tells me before leaving with another ranger on foot patrol. It's a hot August afternoon, but they plan to go all the way from the greenbelt's trailhead at Barton Springs Pool to its far end at the Lost Creek subdivision. And back. The trip can take anywhere from four to seven hours. It all depends on how many people they find along the way who need help or need to be advised of something. On this day after several weeks without rain, Barton Creek has few swimming holes left and the rangers aren't expecting too many people.

It was just the opposite in June when the creek was full and hundreds of area residents, visitors, and tourists were on the greenbelt every day, says Sandra. "Overuse issues are what we're dealing with. The amount of trash at the trailheads is incredible, and sometimes people don't bring up their cans and bottles. We need people to take their stuff away, to put their liquids in water bottles that they'll take home." She says the rangers try to engage people about the fragile nature of the creek environment. Banners reading "Leave No Trace" are hung where the crowds concentrate. They explain that forging new trails off the marked ones only damages the vegetation. They show rock climbers the proper ways to enjoy the sport without permanently defacing the cliffs.

Melissa Hand, a new young ranger from California, tells me she considers the greenbelt "back country," but many users don't see it that way. They hike down with little or no water and then get lost, she says. "I try to educate them about how some of these trails are 'technical' hikes, and the heat can be a real danger." When the greenbelt was closed for several days in 2016 because of flood conditions, signs went up and access gates were closed off. "But I must have talked to a hundred people who said they just hopped over the gates."

7 HIDDEN NEIGHBORS

Famed Author's Retreat and The Nature Conservancy's Preserve

The cougar walked slowly and with purpose. A rabbit scurried ahead of her on a trail and she could smell it. Leading to the old house just above Barton Creek, the trail fronts a lawn that attracts small mammals, deer, turkeys, and birds. Some of the house's occupants take the trail to swim in the creek below where it pools around a rock big enough for jumping or sunbathing. Not long after dawn on a July day, Nan Cuba sat outside on the front porch enjoying her coffee before a run. Swimming in the creek didn't interest her much after spotting a water moccasin undulating through the water in the early days of her residency at the house.

Nan saw the rabbit first. Then her eyes landed on the cougar. It froze just a few yards from where she sat. The cougar looked directly at her and she returned the stare. Three minutes passed before the lean, tawny animal turned around and walked down the trail the way it had come. "I wasn't scared. I had heard a cougar had been spotted on the property before, so it wasn't too much of a surprise," she says when I visit her a few weeks later. "I think it was a female, not too big." The encounter happened not far from where Barton Creek runs close to the teeming shops and roads of the Bee Cave suburb southwest of Austin. Nan, who grew up on a farm near Temple, tells me she was awed to be in the presence of a magnificent animal that very few Central Texans ever see in the wild today.

Like other temporary residents of the house once owned by the famed Texas writer J. Frank Dobie,

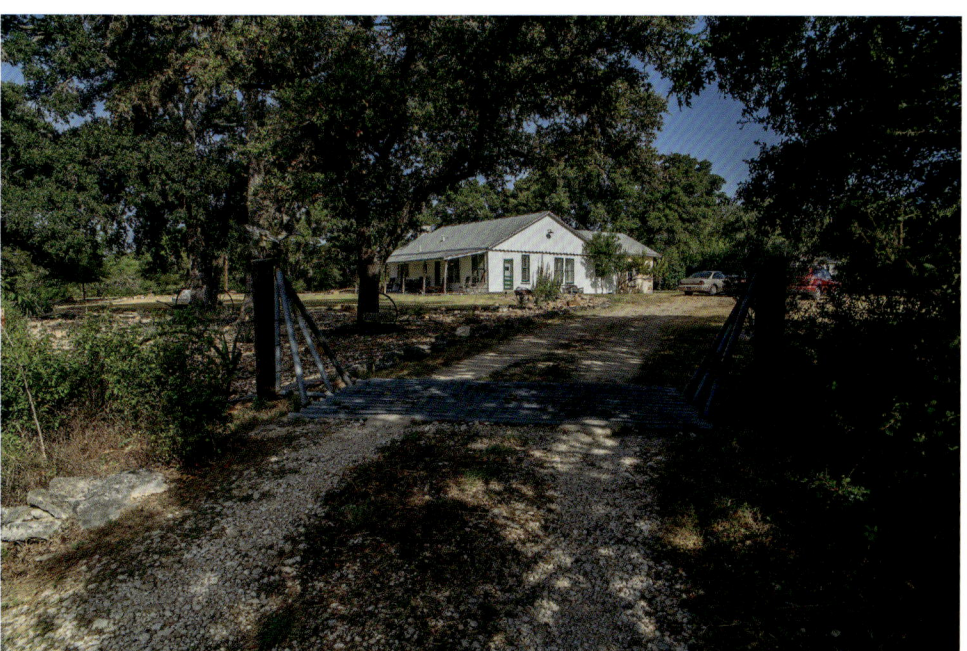

The Paisano writers' retreat is on creek property once owned by J. Frank Dobie.

Nan Cuba of San Antonio observed plenty of wildlife during her stay at Paisano Ranch.

she had been informed she would observe plenty of wildlife during her six-month stay at the University of Texas' fellowship retreat for writers. Michael Adams, director and fund-raiser of the program since 2008 and the determined caretaker of the property, says he has glimpsed the cougar twice. A nearby bluff with dark, cavelike recesses is likely where she resides.

The 254 acres that Dobie dubbed Paisano Ranch, using the Spanish word for the large roadrunner birds, is an oasis of natural wildness. Barton Creek courses through the property from the west and passes the modest white house at the end of a low-water crossing road. Downstream from the house the creek turns under soaring cliffs and offers even more swimming holes shaded by oaks, elms, and sycamores. When Dobie bought the ranch as a getaway in 1959 toward the end of his life, it was way beyond the hubbub of Austin. Paisano was countryside then, fourteen miles from his Austin home near the university campus. The writer described it as "not an estate, not a ranch, not a farm. It is merely a place of some acres in the hills west of Austin."

Today atop the hillsides behind the Dobie house, which was built around a late 1800s log cabin, is tony Bee Cave. Massive homes in the golf course development of Spanish Oaks perch above the retreat and stretch across nearly three miles of hilltops along Texas 71. Shopping malls, condos, and parking lots occupy the highway's frontage acreage. The only way to get to Paisano is by a two-mile-long, mostly gravel private road south of the town. The road starts in a sparsely populated area near the Austin Zoo, where some three hundred rescue animals attract multitudes of kids and parents. No conservation easement exists on the UT-owned property, but conservation lands managed by the City of Austin and The Nature Conservancy nearby give the retreat a feeling of isolation .

Nan Cuba stayed at the ranch in 2016 alone, working at her solitary craft. The wildlife and wildflowers kept her company and soothed her through months of laboring on an absurdist novel based on a real-life serial murderer and an overeager justice system. Henry Lee Lucas had prowled for victims along the highways from Florida to Texas in the 1970s and early 1980s. Nan, a former journalist who teaches at Our Lady of the Lake University in San Antonio, wrote news accounts of his crimes and his exaggerated claims that ended in a life sentence.

She considers herself a nature lover and at Paisano became fond of running on the grassy trails and gravel road. While she drew the line at swimming in the creek populated by fish and frogs, turtles and snakes, she welcomed visitors to do so. I tell her I'll take her up on the offer, but first I want to hear about her past trying weeks at the retreat. The creek flooded repeatedly from heavy rainstorms in May and June. The usually placid water curving through canyons turned into a muddy, raging river. It was well over the low-water crossing to the house, cutting off her only way out of the ranch. Her supplies of food and drinking water were nearly gone. Nan couldn't drive her car out, and no one could drive in across the concrete slab bridge. Two white markers at the crossing measured the depth from one to five feet. They had been topped out, and one was broken.

Michael got a call from Nan for help. He drove

Several feet of floodwaters in 2016 cut off the only road into the retreat.

out to find six feet of torrent over the crossing. He told her he'd have to phone a neighboring property owner to rescue her. Phil Mockford has lived on 225 acres upstream of Paisano since 1978. He's seen many drought-and-flood cycles. "I don't cuss the rain no matter how much comes," he says in deference to nourishment of wells, livestock, grasses and trees, and the aquifer. "I had a little bit of trouble getting my Mule [a small four-wheel Kawasaki vehicle] through the mud to get down to her," Mockford says of his mission to assist the writer. Although his land includes Barton Creek frontage, his house is much higher than Dobie's and has no low-water access to navigate. Nan describes the ride with him as a wild, winding journey through the woods. She had no idea where she was going. Once they got to the neighbor's house, they switched to his pickup truck and "before I knew it I was out on the highway and there was the H-E-B" for groceries.

In early July, Nan needed help a second time. The water-delivery truck still couldn't get to the house to refill the twin backyard tanks that hold drinking water. She was running out of food again. Michael loaded up a couple of backpacks, drove out to the ranch, and made two crossings on foot when the water over the road had receded to knee deep. The wiry English professor, then sixty-nine with two hip replacements, used canes to steady himself in the swift current. His resupply mission succeeded.

When I visit Nan again, the road crossing is dry and the creek's pools are back to normal levels of about four feet. The water is clear and cool to the touch. I can't wait to swim. Alone. In the summer. In Barton Creek. Here, all to myself, is the refreshing gem I had known primarily from crowded downstream spots along the public greenbelt. A big ol' goofy grin spreads across my face as Nan points me to a trail that ends at water's edge. The creek bottom was scrubbed clean by the floods, and the midday sun reflects off the white limestone. The only noticeable signs of tons of rushing water are the squashed clumps of muhly grass and bent or broken saplings.

I swim with eyes wide open, subconsciously scanning for snakes, to the flat-topped boulder sticking out above the middle of the stream. The limestone hunk the size of a car has been eroded and sculpted by centuries of water rushing around and over it. Climbing atop the rock, I startle a couple of red-eared sliders that had been sunning on a ledge. The turtles plop into the water, obviously preferring the company of minnows to a human interloper. The boulder could hold two or three people, but I don't want company. The only sound in what seems like a remote canyon hundreds of miles from civilization is the water. It gurgles and softly splashes around the big rock and smaller ones nearby. Listening to the quiet is something I had almost forgotten how to do.

I wonder if Dobie or his friends enjoyed this spot. But the writer was not in the best of health in the few years he owned Paisano until his death in 1964, so he curtailed his swimming routines then. He had been a frequent swimmer at Barton Springs Pool in the 1950s. Today pool visitors pass a life-sized bronze sculpture of Dobie clad in a bathing suit outside the main entrance.

As a University of Texas professor in the 1930s and 1940s, he authored books and periodicals with folksy tales about the state's renegades, ranchers, and rattlesnakes. Among his friends also depicted in the sculpture are the naturalist Roy Bedichek and Walter Prescott Webb, who chronicled such western institutions as the Texas Rangers. The three often gathered on a limestone ledge along the pool, more to talk and debate than to swim. Their gathering spot, dubbed Conversation Rock, washed away in a flood a few years ago. The rock and its literary trio were immortalized in the sculpture by Glenna Goodacre in 1994 after a group led by Austin writers raised funds for the work. Tourists and Austinites frequently stop in front of the statue for selfies and group photos with the figures. I've taken more than one shot of my grandchildren posing in Dobie's lap. I doubt many of the pool visitors know about the ranch he owned on Barton Creek and that his widow, Bertha, helped the university acquire it.

While Dobie did not write about the creek, A. C. Greene, the second fellow at Paisano after it became a UT retreat in 1967, wrote this eloquent description in a 1969 promotional pamphlet for the fellowship program:

> Barton Creek, still 30 or so twisting miles from its mouth, runs clear and sweet most years. It curls and chatters among the rocks, and whispers into dark, tree hung places and pools where the imagination pictures both delights and dangers. Dominating the natural scenery are massive limestone bluffs which form the pictorial backdrop for views from the front gallery. Here the Canyon Wren's tumbling, crystal song pours out in season, the Chuck-Will's Widow calls through the spring nights. Dripping springs, fern surrounded, chime from the rocks and on rare winter days, icicles form like beards off their ledges.

I call Sarah Bird, who was awarded a Paisano fellowship in 2010, because I know she is an avid swimmer. The Austin novelist says that when she lived at the ranch with her husband in the summer, she swam most every day. "It was so dreamy. I can't tell you the number of hours I spent just lying on my back in the creek. I'd look up and watch the vultures flying overhead and eyeing me." She says there was just the right amount of water flow that summer, neither drought nor flood conditions. "We'd hike around with our two dogs and then swim. And the best thing is that out there you can swim naked. It was ideal, beautiful. Barton Creek was the centerpiece of my time there."

The solitude that Nan enjoyed was interrupted only by one young couple who had canoed down the creek. She came upon them sitting on the big rock midstream. On her walks to a pioneer cabin on the property not far from neighboring construction, "I often heard workers sawing trees and hammering." Michael, the protector of Paisano, worries about all the development above the retreat. He knows that if a couple of owners of large tracts adjacent to the ranch sell out, the quietude for writers could disappear. He's seen how easily the university's land buffer can be damaged.

A midcreek rock at Paisano invites jumps and contemplation.

Michael invites me to take a hike up to the northern property line. We follow a rusted barbed-wire and cedar-post fence that starts just west of the Dobie house. Thickets of cedar trees and patches of prickly pear cactus slow our progress, but Michael leads me to the boundary with the Spanish Oaks development. The sudden appearance through the trees of the large, manicured backyards of a half-dozen houses is jarring. The contrast with Paisano's simplicity overwhelms me. On the ranch's side is the wire fence used decades ago to keep goats from wandering away. Inches beyond stands a new eight-foot-high wrought-iron fence designed to keep strangers out and children and dogs inside.

Some of the soaring villa-style houses with clay-tiled roofs have backed up to the Paisano property for ten years or more. But construction slowed with the development's foreclosure in 2010 and a management restructuring. Lots are being sold again, and Spanish Oaks now stretches across several hillsides and valleys with houses, golf courses, pools, and other recreational facilities. The development encompasses Little Barton Creek, a main tributary that flows into Barton Creek near the Texas 71 bridge.

Following the old fence on Paisano's side, we walk into a clearing an acre and a quarter in size. Except for some oak trees, the site holds only the low native grasses that appear a few seasons after Central Texas ground has been scraped clean. Here and there poke up the sawed-off stumps of large, old-growth cedars. Around Christmastime in 2012, Michael hiked the property line and discovered the devastating work of a bulldozer and chain saws. He was appalled to see that land owned by the university had been so obviously violated. The barbed-wire fence was knocked down behind a new homesite and the land cleared. It was not a whodunit.

"Devastation," he called it at the time. "We're being encroached upon and violated." He quickly reported the destruction to university officials, but six months went by without any action. The university finally hired a surveyor to check the property lines and assess the damage. The professor had the barbed-wire fencing rebuilt and a stone pillar erected on the cleared land facing the development. He hung on the pillar a sign reading "Paisano Ranch. Property of The University of Texas. No trespassing." End of story. Clearly still frustrated that the university declined to seek compensation for the land damage, Michael recalled one former Paisano resident's comment about the incursion: "If somebody tore down the fence at the football field and sawed off their goalpost, if thirty yards of the football stadium were devastated, what would UT have done about it six months later?"

When I visited the site, a new water-retention pond had been built across the fence near where more houses were going up. Downhill from the pond, four culvert pipes buried in a stonework berm point toward the ranch. Rainwater draining from the pond passes through the culverts and into a twenty-foot-long, two-foot-deep concrete trough. If the trough overflows in a heavy rain, the runoff nonetheless will spill onto the Paisano land and head downhill toward Barton Creek. In 2017, the city of Bee Cave approved a one hundred–acre development plan for another section called Hillside at Spanish Oaks. With the land pitched at a steep 25 percent grade in some places, developers nonetheless will put sixty-four houses and sixteen condominiums on the property.

On the east side of Texas 71, built-out developments sit atop the hills above Barton Creek as it winds its way out of Bee Cave. The Uplands and The Preserve at Barton Creek provide some views of the creek, but most of the waterway is inaccessible from those developments thanks to a long-ago battle by environmentalists. In 1990, many more homes were platted in the area. The initial fire hydrants and water lines were installed. Next, trees would be taken out and roads would be scraped into the landscape. But then the developers ran into the uprising of Austin's environmental movement. Had it not been for that—and two rare birds—the land would not be owned and managed today by The Nature Conservancy. Four miles of Barton Creek likely would not be as clean and beautiful as it is today.

Barton Creek Habitat Preserve hides off busy Bee Caves Road, reaching south to Southwest Parkway and split by Texas 71 on the west. The forty-one hundred acres are unknown to most nearby residents because the preserve is not open to the general public. The huge swath of greenery, hills, and Barton Creek is a paradise rescued from the poised blades of bulldozers. I found the preserve by accident while roaming areas along the creek's path downstream of Paisano.

The unassuming entrance, with a locked gate and a small sign noting it is property of The Nature Conservancy, is on a gravel road just a few yards from where residents of a nearby development come and go through a fancier entrance with keypad security. The beautifully wild preserve includes a historic stone cabin that sits above a wide, straight run of the creek. The cabin is used as the preserve's office. Built in 1877, it was the home of Gus Bohls, whose father, Dietrich Bohls, was the earliest white settler in the area in the 1850s. Dietrich's log cabins at the confluence of Barton Creek and Little Barton Creek were restored by the Spanish Oaks developers.

An account of the family in Elaine Perkins's book *A Hill Country Paradise?* says the German immigrant found Austin too crowded with 850 residents and wanted more privacy. The land he chose near the two creeks "provided potable water for the family and plenty of trees available for the building of cabins. Bohls was also sure that the soil along the creek bed

Brandon Crawford manages the forty-one hundred acres of Barton Creek Habitat Preserve.

was fertile enough for growing crops." Indians, not all hostile, roamed the area hunting for deer, turkey, and wild pigs.

Today, Brandon Crawford works on his computer in the cabin as the lone manager of the preserve. He has a large equipment barn in the preserve's interior and brings in helpers from the conservancy as needed. Most of his days are devoted to improving the nesting habitats of the golden-cheeked warblers and black-capped vireos. He keeps native oaks and cedar trees in balance and maintains large areas of lush grasslands. He also maintains a few trails so small groups of scouts, university students, and bird counters can have access to the land by appointment.

Since 2005, the West Texas native with an ecology degree has protected the sprawling acreage and the creek's precious riparian areas. He's increasingly surrounded by new residential and commercial developments. "The bonus of this preserve, which was established for the birds, is the water here," he says. "Barton Creek is fed by dozens of springs on the hillsides and in the creek bed. The previous manager told me the creek would flow clear in just half a day after a major flood. Now it takes much longer for the creek to clean itself up."

On a frigid December day, we take a short hike on a trail from the cabin and stop at one of the crucial springs. From under a boulder and a patch of moss flows a steady stream of water no wider than a handprint. The water picks its way through the brush and down the hill toward the creek. It joins a stronger tributary stream pouring into the creek. "I've never seen this water dry up completely," Brandon says. "There's likely another spring somewhere feeding into this." We wind up on a low-water crossing over the creek where I'm amazed to see such an uncommonly wide and straight stretch of water. At least forty feet across and a quarter-mile long. Above where the creek first appears around a bend to the west, a Tuscan-style house with huge windows hugs the top of a cliff. The private view into the preserve undoubtedly is worth the home's multi-million-dollar price tag.

Brandon says he occasionally comes across intruders, mostly teenagers who slip through the woods to party at the creek. When the water is running high enough, kayakers paddle through the preserve. It's legal if they put in at a public access point upstream and don't wander beyond the banks. He tries to talk positively to the people he runs across, explaining why the bird sanctuary is not a public recreation area like the greenbelt in Austin. Most area residents, he notes, respect the no-trespassing signs posted along the preserve's perimeter fence line. Sometimes he refers unwelcome visitors to The Nature Conservancy's web pages that celebrate the four miles of "peaceful Barton Creek, a crystal-clear stream beloved by Austinites. . . . Guarded on both sides by canyon walls, alternative fast and rocky or deep and contemplative, Barton Creek is Austin's lifeblood . . . and recharges the Edwards Aquifer."

Brandon doesn't like the heavy traffic he must negotiate on his way to and from a job that he loves. It keeps getting worse, he says, and development on every side of the preserve continues unabated as landowners with once-rural acreage sell out. Before this decade ends, he estimates more than 75 percent of the preserve's border fence will be along the backyards of someone's house or business. What's not going to change is the care and respect brought to four miles of Barton Creek midway on its journey toward Austin. As with other conservation lands upstream, the preserve is a healthy and vital part of the aquifer's heartbeat. Brandon intends to keep it that way, reminding neighbors at every opportunity of the responsibility that comes with property near such a treasured creek.

8 VIREOS AND WARBLERS

Working to Keep Thousands of Acres of Habitat Beckoning Birds

What does it take to ensure that two small migrating bird species find attractive nesting spots in the hills west and north of Austin? Thousands of protected acres. Dozens of bird experts, habitat scientists, and maintenance laborers for the city's water-quality protection and water-utility departments. Numerous federal employees of the Balcones Canyonlands National Wildlife Refuge and a host of environmental groups manage other acreage vital to the birds' survival.

Amid hundreds of morning commuters driving to work on Loop 360 south of Lake Austin, I turn off the highway onto an unmarked road into the green hills. The 214-acre Vireo Preserve is in the middle of a big bend of the Colorado River where upscale housing developments have proliferated over the past few decades. City of Austin biologists who study the visiting black-capped vireo and golden-cheeked warbler are going to show me the habitats that exist here with the help of specific land-management practices. Neither myself nor photographer Alberto Martinez is likely

Protected land for endangered birds lies across Lake Austin from downtown.

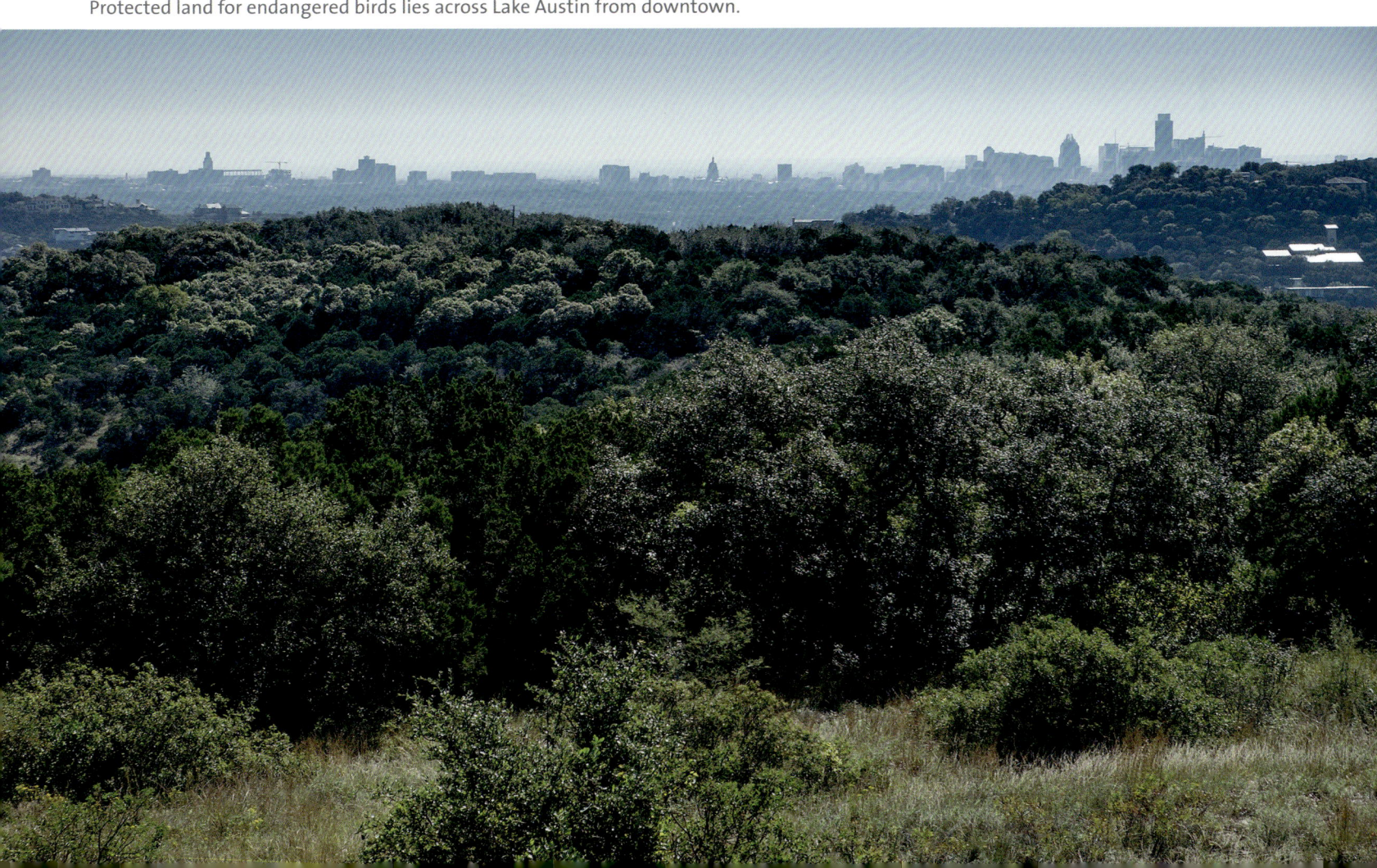

to see a vireo unless a pair has overstayed their usual migration and nesting season here. By fall the parents and young offspring have left their nests to winter on the western coast of Mexico. Lucky birds, I'm thinking.

Lisa and Jim O'Donnell, biologists for the city, meet us wearing their matching gold wedding bands sculpted with vireos and shin oak leaves. Another biologist and bird expert accompanying us is Bill Reiner, also a city biologist. All of them are involved in managing the habitats and chronicling the comings and goings of the birds. The land adjoins Wild Basin, a Travis County–owned preserve created in the 1970s. Both tracts are part of the much larger Balcones Canyonlands Preserve system. Unlike many of the other Balcones lands, Wild Basin's 227 acres are open to the public for hiking. St. Edward's University operates an education and research center there as well. The O'Donnells help manage the bird habitat at Wild Basin. Both properties were the scene of a major fire in 1961 that changed the landscape entirely. Once overgrazed by goats and cleared of old-growth cedar trees used for lumber, the land was a virtual wasteland of exposed caliche soil and scrub vegetation. After the fire, new growth of grasses and hardwood trees, plus soil restoration, resulted in today's balanced woodlands and grasslands.

The acreage drains into the Bee Creek and Lake Austin watersheds. It shares a now-inescapable problem with Barton Creek Habitat Preserve to the west—development has encircled the preserves. The migrating populations of vireos and warblers apparently noticed that hubbub and the ever-rising downtown skyline to the east. The numbers of birds counted, especially the vireo, collapsed as urbanization spread in the late 1980s. Many of the vireos now nest farther west and north in Texas. It will be hard to get them back here so close to metropolitan housing and traffic, but the Balcones biologists are trying their damnedest. They even tried attacking an enemy nest robber to improve the situation.

The future for the vireo, which breeds only in low-growth habitat in Texas, Oklahoma, and northernmost Mexico, looked bleak in decades past. Only about 350 birds were known to survive in a few locations. Following the bird's listing under the Endangered Species Act in 1987 and with recovery efforts, there are now more than 5,200 known birds and more than 14,000 estimated across their breeding range, according to federal officials. The warbler, more colorful than the black-and-white vireo with its bright yellow head, nests exclusively in the mature oak-juniper woodlands of Central Texas. The loss of that specific habitat has taken a 25 percent toll on the songbird since its listing as endangered in 1990. The federal government estimates a current population of 27,000.

Two Protected Central Texas Birds

Golden-cheeked warbler (*Setophaga chrysoparia*)
Listed under the Endangered Species Act in 1990, the songbird has brilliant yellow cheeks (less bright in females) outlined in black and a thin black line through each eye. The underside of the body is white with some black markings and blackish wings. Of more than five hundred species of birds found in Texas, the warbler is the only one that breeds exclusively in the state. It is about five inches long, with an eight-inch wingspan. The warblers winter in the highlands of Mexico and Central America.

Black-capped vireo (*Vireo atricapilla*)
Listed under the Endangered Species Act in 1987 and delisted in 2018, the songbird has a black head (gray in females) with white around its reddish eyes. The body has an olive back and a whitish belly. The wing markings are pale yellow. It nests only in Central and Southwest Texas and in central Oklahoma. About four and a half inches long with a seven-inch wingspan, the bird winters in Mexico. The US Fish and Wildlife Service will monitor populations for twelve years.

Both birds benefited from a confluence of events and interests at the end of the 1980s. Developers were trying to climb out of a debt canyon after the failure of savings and loans across the country, with more than half of the S&L losses occurring in Texas. The Resolution Trust Corporation was created to try to sell off some of the S&Ls' foreclosed lands. Central Texas was fortunate because it was attracting new high-tech businesses and its economy had not suffered from the 1986 oil-price bust as much as other areas of the state. Environmentalists here felt empowered with the Endangered Species Act, amended in 1988 to strengthen recovery plans for protected species.

Golden-cheeked warbler. (Photo by Greg Lasley)

Black-capped vireo. (Photo by Greg Lasley)

Once the vireo and the warbler had endangered status, their protectors started looking for habitat lands they could acquire. Austin and Travis County passed bonds to buy acreage held by the Resolution Trust Corporation. Groups such as The Nature Conservancy sought out purchases as well. Deals with developers were made to get other lands through environmental mitigation—essentially allowing developers to build on some tracts they owned in exchange for more environmentally sensitive land in other areas. The biggest result of these maneuvers was the Balcones Canyonlands Conservation Plan of 1992. The multiagency effort established the 27,500-acre Balcones Canyonlands National Wildlife Refuge north of Lake Travis in Burnet and Travis Counties. Piece by piece, other lands along the Colorado River and reaching south to Barton Creek were acquired or put under conservation easements by Travis County, the City of Austin, The Nature Conservancy, the National Audubon Society, and private landowners. Those tracts amounted to more than thirty-one thousand acres, of which about thirteen thousand acres are managed as endangered bird habitat.

Lisa O'Donnell says that in 1987 when she first came out to the land we are walking through, there were vireo territories everywhere. "It was hard to imagine this place without them. Then the decline happened fairly quickly. In 2010, we started trying different practices under our federal [endangered species] permit to manipulate the habitat and stop it from becoming too forested. The root systems were old and good, so we basically gave it a haircut with chainsaws and other hand tools and mulched it up. That didn't damage the soil."

We enter a fenced-off nursery and pollination area, where master naturalist volunteers get plants and trees started before transplanting. Nearby, a two hundred–gallon rainwater collection tank is one of four on the property used to nourish the young plants. "One thing we do differently than some land managers is we build from the soil up," says Jim O'Donnell as we walk out along a hillside that once was only bare caliche and cedar. Volunteers and preserve workers cut the cedar first. Then they wield pitchforks to aerate the soil, adding organic matter and mulch. "It works out very well. A US Department of Agriculture study found that for every one percent of organic matter added to the soil per acre, it captures an additional twenty-five thousand gallons of water." He points out the cut cedar branches and trunks arranged in berms along the contours of the hillside to slow and pool rainfall runoff. Little bluestem grass seed was sown between plantings of persimmon, shin oak, Spanish oak, live oak, and yaupon. The result today is an inviting habitat with the bushy growth that vireos favor.

The birds build their nests about three feet off the ground. They want enough foliage to hide their nests, constructed with grass, leaves, and bark. Sticky spider silk is gathered to hold the nests together and secure them to the forks of branches. Jim pulls back the outer stems and leaves of a chest-high yaupon to show me an ideal spot for a nest.

We walk downhill to a denser area of fat cedars and tall Spanish oaks. Bill Reiner says both are prime components of golden-cheeked warbler habitat. The birds pull thin strips of bark from the mature cedars for their nest building. The warblers nest fifteen to thirty feet high in the oaks. They feed themselves and their young from the trees' populations of beetles, caterpillars, moths, and katydids. Bill spreads open some cedar branches to find oak sprouts beneath the low tangles of branches. "These sprouts are protected from deer that otherwise would eat them in the open. They also grow better in the dappled sunlight that gets through the cedars instead of baking in full sun." It's the kind of symbiotic relationship that Bill obviously enjoys explaining.

One reason that most of the Balcones habitat lands are not open to the public, Jim adds, is that deer

Biologist Jim O'Donnell reaches into hidden habitat for vireo nests.

need to be regularly culled on them to protect the plant life and, in turn, the birds. Hunting can't be done safely where the public is allowed on protection lands such as the Barton Creek greenbelt and Emma Long Park on Lake Austin. Thus, deer overpopulation and the lack of diversified vegetation from deer munching are challenges there. Deer hunting also is not possible on the birds' habitat land I'm visiting because of the proximity of houses, including the large Davenport Ranch development.

Another unwanted animal on the Balcones preserves is a stocky blackbird called the brown-headed cowbird. The nest stealer is a serious threat to the vireo populations. Instead of building their own nests, the cowbirds lay their eggs in the vireos' nests. Sometimes the adult cowbirds nudge the vireo eggs out of the nest. The cowbird chicks usually hatch first and, because the vireo chicks are smaller, the bigger cowbird mouths get fed more. Sometimes the young vireos starve to death. No wonder the biologists built big cages to trap and eliminate the cowbirds. Bill walks us to one of four that were used for years and talks about a study in Kerr County that found only a 2 percent nest success rate for the vireo young. After cowbird trapping was employed there, that rate climbed to 90 percent.

He says the cowbirds were once "steadfast followers of bison, depending on them for the seeds in their droppings and eating the insects on them. Bison roam so much that the cowbirds couldn't build and maintain nests because then they'd lose their meal ticket. So they learned how to deposit their eggs in the nests of other birds and have those birds raise their young. Now we have stationary bison—they're called cattle. The cowbirds have no reason to move, and their numbers are skyrocketing every place cattle are being raised."

Adds Jim: "I used to come out here and regularly find a vireo nest, but there was often a cowbird egg in it. A cowbird takes about ten days to hatch out, where a vireo takes fourteen to seventeen days. They're already growing fast before the vireos hatch. Sometimes we would catch fifty cowbirds at a time in our traps."

The old cage I'm led to is surprisingly big—built with two-by-fours and chicken-coop wire covered with hardware cloth in a rectangle the size of a U-Haul

Large cages trapped cowbirds to stop them from robbing the nests of vireos.

truck. In the top is a vented trap-door opening. A few male and female cowbirds are trapped in mist nets, fine-meshed nylon strung between two poles like a volleyball net. The entangled cowbirds are put into the cage with food and water and perches. Other cowbirds fly over, land nearby, and watch the attractions inside the cage. Led by strong flocking instincts, they squeeze through the small rooftop vent with wings folded. Trapped, they can't fly out with wings spread. "We called it the Hotel California because, like the Eagles' song, they could never leave," Jim says. Cowbirds are not as much of a problem in golden-cheeked warbler habitat because the warbler young are not so tiny. Both can hatch in a nest and be fed to fledgling size.

As we head back to the preserve's entrance road, the biologists hear a spotted towhee call somewhere overhead. They don't spot it but they know what it is. "That's my first towhee!" Lisa exclaims with joy. She means this season, since it is mid-October and the beginning of the Texas wintering for the birds that migrate from the cold Rocky Mountains regions.

I ask how I'll know if I hear a vireo or a warbler. Bill whips out his cell phone and punches up songbird recordings. "It's a very complex repertoire," he says, as the sound of a black-capped vireo plays. "They have many different songs and phrases they can sing in whatever whim of an order they like. They can sing for a half hour, an hour at a time. Some people describe it as rushed or angry." It sounds shrill and high pitched to me, but Bill says it is not nearly as high pitched as songs of some other songbirds.

What does a golden-cheeked warbler sound like? "It's not as diverse, but it's pretty much the same song as the vireo," he says. "It's sweeter and higher pitched. Think of the songs 'La Cucaracha' or 'Lazy Daisy.'" I can't make the song connections when he plays a sampler, but it does not sound much different than the vireo, only simpler. I confess to the keen-eared biologists that I love the wonderful sounds of songbirds, but I can't whistle the tunes.

Lisa has worked for the City of Austin since 2001, about half of the years in the Watershed Protection Department and now with the Water Utility Department, which manages many of the Balcones preserves. Before that, for ten years, she worked for the US Fish and Wildlife Service and helped write the proposed and final rules for safeguarding the endangered salamanders of Barton Springs. Unlike the salamanders, the golden-cheeked warbler has had to survive challenges by state officials in recent years to its protection under the Fish and Wildlife Service. In 2015, Texas Comptroller Susan Combs, on behalf of a group called Texans for Positive Economic Policy, petitioned Fish and Wildlife to delist the warbler. The effort was unsuccessful, and the service responded that the species "has not been recovered, and due to ongoing, widespread destruction of its habitat, the species continues to be in danger of extinction throughout its range."

The National Audubon Society came to the bird's defense as well that year. David Yarnold, president of the society, wrote: "The golden-cheeked warbler is all Texan. It cannot breed and raise its young anywhere else in the world except the magnificent Texas Hill Country. . . . But the warbler's nesting grounds—those beautiful natural places that make the Hill Country famous—are being eroded, subdivision by subdivision, and building by building, in the 33 counties where it nests. That's why the US Fish and Wildlife Service decided to provide special protections for the golden-cheeked warbler a quarter of a century ago. Even with those legal protections, an estimated 1.5 million acres (nearly a third of the golden-cheeked warbler's home range) disappeared between 1999 and 2011."

The warbler was in headlines and on newscasts again in 2017. In June, the conservative Texas Public Policy Foundation filed a lawsuit to delist the bird from its endangered species status on behalf of the Texas General Land Office headed by George P. Bush. "The restoration of the golden-cheeked warbler population is a success story worth celebrating by removing it from the endangered list and restoring the rights of Texas landowners to effectively manage our own properties," Bush said in a statement from his office.

Fish and Wildlife responded with a court motion to dismiss the Land Office's claims. The warbler still faces ongoing threats because of its dwindling and limited habitats, the agency said. By the fall of 2018, the lawsuit was still unresolved. Lisa says, "I don't think they [the Land Office] are going to back down. They'll keep coming at it."

Meanwhile, the black-capped vireo was delisted by Fish and Wildlife. The agency said regular surveys in Texas (Fort Hood and Kerr Wildlife Management Area) and Oklahoma (Fort Sill and Wichita Mountain Wildlife Refuge) showed stable or increasing populations of the vireo since 2005. "Conservation actions implemented on publicly managed and private lands throughout the species' current range have reversed black-capped vireo declines," the agency said. In a draft of a post-delisting monitoring plan, Fish and Wildlife said it will continue to work with partners, including the Texas Parks and Wildlife Department, Oklahoma Department of Wildlife Conservation, The Nature Conservancy, and the US Army. The plan is estimated to cost $3.7 million over a twelve-year period to ensure "continued recovery of the black-capped vireo so as not to require relisting the species." Lisa says she was disappointed in the delisting because "it feels like they [Fish and Wildlife] circumvented the ongoing recovery plan." She says all parts of the Balcones Canyonlands Preserve system will carry on habitat improvement and maintenance efforts for both the vireo and the warbler.

I leave the preserve acreage off Loop 360, surrounded by urban sprawl, knowing my chances of spotting a nesting vireo or warbler parent come spring will be better on more outlying Balcones lands. Nonetheless, I'm happy that Lisa, Jim, and Bill will keep up their work here to entice any birds looking for a quiet, lush oasis amid the houses and highways.

Evidence of encroachment of the human kind hits Brandon Crawford nearly each time he nears the perimeter of the birds' preserve he manages for The Nature Conservancy on Barton Creek. Right over the fence line is an urbanized landscape that neither the vireo nor the warbler would want to visit. Behind the wheel of a big, well-used pickup, Brandon shows me several sections of the forty-one hundred–acre Barton Creek Habitat Preserve. We pass one of thirteen fire hydrants put in place in the beginning of the 1990s when this land was platted for development and water lines were buried. The conservancy rescued the Bee Cave property before roads and houses could be built.

I ask him about the bird numbers here. He says the golden-cheeked warbler has held to about fifty to eighty breeding pairs over the years since the preserve was created in 1994. "We have a beautiful, stable habitat for them here," he boasts. The uncommon warbler migrates to Central Texas from Central America to mate, nest, and feed its young. This refuge is an island amid development just west of Austin. Not that I expect to see many of the warblers in the middle of June. The visitors arrive around the middle of March and leave by the end of June. For their nest building, the warblers like a fifty-fifty mix of old-growth cedar (Ashe juniper) and mature oaks with dense, insect-populated canopies. I stare at the bigger trees I pass, hoping to spot the bird's distinguishing patch of yellow on the cheeks and around the eyes.

Brandon tells me I almost definitely will not see a black-capped vireo. Although the rare birds arrive here from Mexico's upper Pacific coast in late March to the middle of May and stay through August or sometimes September, their numbers are few at the preserve. The highest count has been fourteen, and the lowest, zero. In the past ten years that he's been managing the habit, Brandon says, the range has been four to zero. Still, I stare intently into the bushes as we drive through a lush meadow. The vireos have a gray and white body, with a darker gray or black head and yellowish cast in their wing and tail feathers. What both

Just outside Barton Creek Habitat Preserve, a neighbor learns from the preserve's manager why access is restricted.

birds face at the preserve is potential habitat loss, says Brandon. "They don't like disturbances and noises. We've lost some acres of what could be habitat here because of all the development and traffic around us."

Brandon does far more at the preserve than drive around looking for the endangered birds. To manage the habitat, he takes out some young growth and oversees prescribed burns to keep the right balance of trees and grasslands. He and part-time helpers from The Nature Conservancy mow a twenty-foot strip along perimeter fence lines where houses back up to the preserve. The preserve, closed to the general public, allows limited white-tailed deer hunts in the interior area by winners of a statewide lottery. Six hunters are each given three-day hunts in the fall to help keep the deer population in check at fewer than four hundred.

One of our first stops after we drive across Barton Creek is Brandon's equipment barn. The large Quonset hut is filled with mowers, tractors, four-wheeler patrol and survey vehicles, saws, and other tools. Parked outside is a small fire truck with a 280-gallon water tank. Crawford and other conservancy workers are trained in conducting prescribed burns and ways to extinguish natural brush fires. He points to a long, gorgeous meadow of little bluestem grass (native) and some King Ranch bluestem (invasive) that reaches out from the front of the barn and covers 125 acres. Much of it was renewed with a prescribed burn a year earlier. Nothing black remains after the grasses, and some mature oaks have greened out.

I want to see how close houses have been built just outside the preserve. These neighborhoods would have been many times larger had the preserve land not been made available as part of a mitigation settlement in the wake of the Barton Creek PUD project rejection by the Austin City Council in 1990. We drive uphill toward where Barton Creek takes a turn underneath the Texas 71 highway. Brandon stops just a few yards short of a rocky ledge overlooking the creek two hundred feet below. "We're at Celena's Overlook," he says. "This is where I proposed to my wife in 2009 and named it for her."

The view is a magnificent valley of light green canopies (oak) and darker green treetops (cedar) separated by the blue ribbon of the creek. "You're looking down on perfect warbler habitat," he says of the old-growth area. Across the canyon and atop the bluffs loom the rooftops of large, expensive houses.

"There are now more houses closer to us," he notes as we head back to the truck for a short drive to the west. We stop at one of his perimeter-clearing sites and walk along the mowed pathway beside a tall barbed-wire fence. We are at the end of a cul-de-sac in The Preserve at Barton Creek, a development described in one realtor's pitch as having "the distinction of being bordered on three sides by the 4,000-acre Barton Creek Habitat Preserve."

As I stare at the startling sight of trimmed lawns and shrubbery, circular driveways, and clay-tiled roofs, a man out walking his two Doberman pinschers comes up to the other side of the fence. "Hello, are you from the preserve?" he asks. Brandon introduces himself as the preserve manager and says he is just checking the condition of the perimeter clearing. The man replies that he lives on a nearby street and likes having the greenery of the preserve.

"What I really want to know," he says, "is if your land could ever become another development or a Wal-Mart?" Brandon explains to him that The Nature Conservancy holds the conservation easement on the preserve "in perpetuity—which means forever." "I'm

Fire hydrants and water lines in place, the preserve was once slated for development.

happy to hear that," says the resident of just a couple of years. "It's very nice that it's all protected. I'm glad I found this neighborhood, where our homes are surrounded by these woods." He introduces himself as Randy English. "I enjoy the sounds out here—coyotes howling, road runners making that clicking sound. We have a great horned owl in our backyard. But I didn't like finding a coral snake in my pool." Brandon tells him about the preserve's primary purpose of protecting the habitat for two rare bird species. He also says he keeps a clearing between the properties as a fire break and so trees don't grow over the fencing. We say our good-byes and head for Vireo Hill.

On the drive to the hill along Southwest Parkway, Brandon talks about the difficulties of being surrounded by more and more housing developments. "They think of it as just a bunch of trees over here. They don't know about the birds, and they think my fencing [most of it old barbed wire] means nothing. Some people even tear it down and put in gates on their fences." He says the trespassers are often teenagers but sometimes their parents as well. "I try to explain to them the liability issues. This is rough land. If they fall and break a leg, or get bit by a rattlesnake, or if a fire got started. . . ." He says he has tried notifying homeowners' associations of the preserve's mission and that the bird sanctuary is not public land. But he's not sure if the word is getting out, and perhaps, he says, he needs to send hundreds of letters to all the homeowners. Later, I spot an online pitch for the Santal apartments off Southwest Parkway: "At our brand new Austin apartments you can enjoy the fresh air on your morning walk through the Barton Creek Habitat Preserve."

We take a winding dirt road up what the conservancy has named Vireo Hill. Like many of the peaks in this area, it is an elongated ridgeline of what once was a cattle ranch on the outskirts of Austin. An old windmill still stands near the base. Brandon isn't certain how high we are at the summit, but he knows where the US Geological Survey elevation marker lies. He brushes aside dirt and grass to read it: 980 feet. "A couple of hills in the preserve are higher," he says as we walk to the east side of the ridge. "But this is the best view." I ask him if vireos do indeed nest up on this namesake hill. "Yes, over the years it's had one of the biggest populations." We can see for miles, and for the first time I get a sense of how much green space there is in the preserve. The outline of where Barton Creek curves around the preserve for four miles is discernible from here. The intense green color of the creek's valleys and the white of the creek's limestone bluffs are a giveaway even though I can't see the water.

I also can tell where the preserve's twenty-one miles of perimeter lie by following the rooftops on the horizons. Houses, apartment buildings, churches, and office buildings loom above the green along Bee Caves Road and, increasingly, along Southwest Parkway. Still, it's nearly breathtaking for me to imagine what the view would be like without the preserve. Brandon also thinks about that whenever he's atop Vireo Hill. "Every time a new house or building pops up, I think it's on our land. It's not of course, but it's awfully close. I'm surrounded now." He stands alone for a while just looking at the preserve he knows so well after more than a decade as its manager. I tell him it must make him feel proud to protect this habitat for two vulnerable wild creatures. "I do treat it like it's mine. I'm so lucky and feel chosen to take care of it the best I can. It's a big responsibility that I take very seriously."

9 CHECKING FOR POLLUTANTS

Watershed Checkups amid New Pressures from Development

It's not unusual to see scientists in creek-wading gear coming and going from the warren of small offices on the eleventh floor of One Texas Center in downtown Austin. They are pollutant monitors for the city's Watershed Protection Department who regularly get wet looking for bugs and other vital signs of the health of area creeks. They are like physicians with their forceps, specimen bottles, measurement tools, analysis devices, and computers. I was eager to step into their outdoor examination rooms and see what they do where on Barton Creek. The creek's watershed is one of forty-nine that are surveyed by the department on a two-year rotating basis. The same sites are sampled four times during each visitation year. The physician analogy goes only so far. The monitors examine the water but don't treat it on the spot if it's ailing. They do sound an alarm, though, and urgent issues such as a large bloom of algae or a chemical spill would be answered by city cleanup crews and investigators.

My appointment is to meet the stream monitors early on a May morning at their offices and go wading with them for the day. The team leader is Staryn Wagner; accompanied by fellow environmental scientists Mateo Scoggins and Chris Herrington; and Sarah Donelson, an instructor for the department's Earth Camp for youths. We're all wearing water shoes

Measurement devices record flow and bank conditions for the Environmental Integrity Index.

and wading clothes. The plan is to visit four sites on Barton Creek upstream of Austin—the Stark family's former sports camp, the Shield Ranch conservation land, a spot under the Texas 71 highway bridge, and a residence off Bee Caves Road. These sites have been sampled for more than two decades.

The creek examinations are to collect data for the Environmental Integrity Index (EII), the department's scorecard for watershed health. Six of the creeks regularly surveyed flow, in part, over the Barton Springs segment of the Edwards Aquifer recharge zone. That means the watersheds of Barton, Onion, Williamson, Slaughter, Bear, and Little Bear Creeks are critical for replenishing the aquifer with clean water that will come up in Barton Springs. I had heard of the EII but had no idea how the index was compiled. After the scientists stash their gear in a big city pickup truck, we're off to make the rounds they know well.

Our first stop is a familiar one to me on Bell Springs Road northwest of Dripping Springs. Staryn punches in the gate code to the property of Richard and Susan Stark. I had already visited the Starks to get their story of life on Barton Creek since 1969, when they bought twenty-two acres for their home and the Sports Country Camp. The youth camp closed in 2015, but the couple still live there. They've welcomed EII crews since the mid-1990s when a city biologist who was the father of campers asked if he could do surveys there.

Though the property is well beyond Austin's extraterritorial jurisdiction for development controls, the city wants to know if any pollutants are coming downstream from that far out. The Starks are just outside Dripping Springs' ETJ. The Texas legislature has declined to give counties zoning powers in unincorporated areas, so almost anything could be built near the Starks' pretty piece of Hays County land and, perhaps, have an impact on Barton Creek's water quality. (Susan Stark says the only problem she recalls is an algae bloom thought to have been caused by cattle upstream.)

Andrew Clamann, a biologist with Austin's Watershed Protection Department, applied a medical analogy of his own in explaining why and where the city does EII surveys:

It's kind of like a doctor trying to evaluate your cholesterol level. He can take a blood sample and tell you that it's currently high or low, but having a record over time is much more meaningful. It helps establish trends and clues for diagnosis. Since our jurisdiction is the receiving water, it is important to know the chemical, physical, and biological characteristics of the headwaters even if it's beyond our borders.

When the EII team arrives at the Starks' property below their house, no one disturbs the couple. Parking near a shaded bank of the creek, the scientists quickly get to work. Staryn calls out the starting time, and the synchronized EII team wades into the water with iPads, nets, white steel pans, and measuring equipment. Staryn suggests I use one of the iPads to punch in the creek bank size, water depth, and velocity numbers that Chris Herrington will collect, but I don't want any part of possibly dropping city electronic property in the water. Instead, I volunteer to hold the stream-flow velocity stick, a calibrated, four-foot steel rod with a rubber pressure cup above a metal disk that rests on the creek bottom.

Chris, who doubles for the department as a legislation watcher during sessions of the Texas legislature, picks out where to take his first measurement. I learn that streams generally have three parts: pool (a deep calm area), run (the normal flowing part), and riffle (the bubbling movement over rocks or other obstructions). A run is where we tie a big spooled-out yellow tape measure across the top of the water to record for the EII the creek's width from bank to bank. Then we stand in the creek behind the tape on the downstream side so as not to disrupt the flow. I move the velocity rod to ten intervals across the width of the creek as Chris checks the small readout box attached to his waist and wired to the rod. He punches the numbers into his iPad and tells me this is a steady, moderate flow. (The team doesn't go out soon after floods, waiting instead until conditions return to normal. In a drought, the scientists search the sites for wherever there is running water.)

While we do our width and flow measurements, Mateo Scoggins and Sarah Donelson search riffles for diatoms (a type of algae) and benthic macroinvertebrates (water bugs). Riffles, where the water is most oxygenated, is where the greatest number of organisms usually are found. Algae are scraped off rocks. To get some bugs, they scoop up water in shallow white pans that make it easier to spot the tiny, dark-colored critters. They also gently turn over rocks on the creek bottom to search for more bugs, holding nets at the ready. "The bugs have a strong evolutionary move of going downstream if they're disturbed," says Mateo. Once caught, the bugs are sorted and put into sampling bottles with small, blunt forceps. At this site about 200 are kept and about 250 are returned to the water. The larval populations of mayflies, caddisflies, and stoneflies will be identified and analyzed back at the department's lab.

The find of the day on this outing, at least sizewise, is a large (over an inch) hellgrammite larva, sometimes called a dobsonfly. It looks to me like a fat centipede with pincers. Mateo says the bug populations change with the seasons, the amount of flow in the creek, and the amount of pollutants in the water. Generally, he says, a sizable number of bugs means a healthy creek. While I help on stream-flow duty, Staryn wades upstream with a mirrorlike densiometer to quantify the amount of tree canopy shading the stream. He also takes water-quality spot measurements (temperature, conductivity, dissolved oxygen, pH) with a multiprobe sonde.

After we complete measurements on the Starks' property, we visit the three other EII sites downstream on Barton Creek. Next is the Shield Ranch, conser-

City biologist Todd Jackson shows students how to net bugs from riffles in the creek.

CHECKING FOR POLLUTANTS : 85

vation-easements protected land off Hamilton Pool Road, which feels vast as we drive to the sampling site on the six miles of creek. At the third stop, we park along Texas 71 and walk under the Barton Creek bridge as cars and trucks roar above going to and fro in Bee Cave. This is where Little Barton Creek joins the main stream below the sprawling Spanish Oaks development. Our final stop is at a gated residence off Bee Caves Road where the turquoise creek winds amid islands of trees behind a couple's house. An old metal ladder leads down to a swimming hole.

At each stop, samples and measurements were taken with practiced dispatch. Returning to their offices late in the day, the wet and muddied scientists talk about issues in the Barton Creek watershed. They worry mostly about erosion from new construction and runoff from new developments (carrying pet waste, fertilizers and pesticides, and vehicle leakage). They also worry about sewage treatment plant malfunctions and the amount of treated effluent sprayed on green spaces.

The watershed department puts it this way in an official description of what the scientists look for: "The field data, pH, dissolved oxygen (DO), temperature and conductivity are collected to describe the characteristics of the stream. If the results of these five characteristics are outside of the expected range, it could indicate a source of pollution. Water samples are analyzed for E. coli bacteria, turbidity, total suspended solids and nutrients. E. coli bacteria are present in creeks at low levels from wildlife, but high levels can indicate contamination from sewage, pets, livestock or humans. . . . High levels of nutrients can come from fertilizers and wastewater contamination and can cause water quality problems including algae blooms and fish kills."

The good news at the end of 2017 is that the EII draft results show Barton Creek is still in excellent condition. Andrew Clamann tells me the scores reflect "one of the benefits of a large watershed that is mostly spring fed and has low concentrations of development in the headwaters—the stream is able to maintain its ability to buffer small changes. Large undeveloped tracts and areas protected from development such as the Shield Ranch maintain a consistency of hydrology and water quality." He says the biological data measure up to those of other recent years. "Barton reliably has great biology due to the perennial flow from cold/clear springs. The diversity and quantity of good water-quality indicator insects such as mayflies, stoneflies, and caddisflies is unparalleled in Austin watersheds. Overall, the biology as reflected by the bugs is really outstanding. The diversity is high, the community structure is balanced, and there are many invertebrate species in the Barton samples that would be intolerant to poor conditions."

I ask what a concerned citizen could eyeball on the creek as indicators that development is beginning to cause trouble. He says more impervious cover near the creek could make it flashy, which means it would rapidly increase in flow shortly after a precipitation event. The result would be erosion of the banks, with soil and vegetation sloughed off and carried downstream. Also, "although algal blooms in the late winter/early spring are somewhat natural, a concerned citizen could look for signs of algal blooms during other times of year, which may indicate increases in nutrients from fertilizer, livestock/pet waste, or even wastewater contamination. I would expect that over time the data will reflect an increase in bacteria and nutrients as the watershed becomes increasingly suburban."

In 2015, Barton Creek scored the highest water quality overall of all the creeks surveyed. The Watershed Protection Department put this notice on its website:

> Barton made a big splash this year, scoring among the highest in the categories of water quality, habitat, aquatic life, contact recreation and non-contact recreation. Although the sediment scores were lower than several other watersheds, it is not surprising

because the lower half of the watershed flows through an urban area. Several pollutants (such as fertilizers, pesticides and petroleum-based chemicals) that are commonly found in urbanized areas adhere to sediment particles. The rain that falls on our roads, houses and yards carries pollutants to the creek. . . . So the next time you see Barton Creek, give her a congratulatory smile and a wave!

Future biologists who might one day conduct EII surveys on area creeks are introduced to the methodology every year by the city's watershed scientists. In February 2018, I watch as Todd Jackson, a biologist for the department, schools forty-five University of Texas students who've caravanned to Barton Creek in the Lost Creek subdivision. Most of them are freshmen in environmental science classes. Jackson wastes no time leading them into riffles in the creek below where a road connects the aging subdivision to a golf course. He shows them how to net invertebrate specimens and sort through their catches to identify them. He demonstrates how to use the equipment to measure stream flow. Jackson explains that "the more bugs living in the creek the better. This is one measure of how healthy the water is here." He's delighted when the students find plenty of the tiny, squiggly creatures.

I return to the watershed department offices not long after the EII survey trip to get a big-picture view of what the future might hold for the health of Barton Creek and other area watersheds. David Johns, geologist program manager and a department employee since 1989, knows well the dangers and possible impact on the aquifer of increasing development. He also recognizes that clean, clear water makes Austin special.

Growing up in Beaumont, I knew if you jumped in the Neches River, you couldn't see your hand or even your belly underwater. To come here and have these natural creek pools where you can see tens of feet down

With forceps, University of Texas students separate and identify creek invertebrates.

to the bottom of these channels was stunning. The reason why the water is so clear is you don't have a lot of suspended solids with organic and mineral debris. And the limestone bedrock, without clay or heavy silt, doesn't trap solids. The water is incredibly clear with low nutrients.

Without many nutrients to chew on, algae stay under control in Barton Creek. But if fed excessive amounts of phosphorus (fertilizers and pesticides) and nitrogen (pet or human waste and fertilizers) via runoff, algae can bloom into stream-choking proportions. Fish kills can result, and the water can be toxic to humans and pets.

David recalls an incident years ago when a holding pond for treated-sewage effluent on a Barton Creek tributary overflowed after a valve broke and thousands of gallons of effluent poured into the creek. "As you walked up the creek, there were enormous sheets of green algae that could be lifted like a blanket, whereas upstream of that the creek was perfectly clear." Accidental spills aside, the quality of the water in Barton Creek reflects what's going on with the land around it, he says. The soils are thin and can easily be eroded. If native grasses and trees rooted solidly over decades get replaced by construction of roads and buildings, rains bring fast runoff instead of slow absorption into the soil.

David describes the scenario over time: "The initial phase of putting in a subdivision tears up the ground for utility lines and roads grading. That's like a one thousand or ten thousand years' equivalent of natural erosion. Then it's sometimes decades before a full build-out of all the houses. Construction may take place during a dry period and nothing much happens, but then when it rains, a lot of bad things can happen in a very short time. Builders' sediment erosion controls often don't work."

Will the recent history of Barton Creek as an unpolluted stream change with the new growth occur-

Envisioned fourteen years ago, Headwaters is building one thousand homes in hills above Barton Creek.

ring outside Austin's jurisdiction? The only certainty is that the type of subdivisions is different now. "A lot of the original development was large-acreage lots, but now more dense developments will impact what happens downstream," David says of the northern Hays County growth. "Water availability was a limiting factor out there ten years ago. If you had a well and a septic tank, regulations specified you had to have a certain amount of acreage. But now that the Lower Colorado River Authority has brought water lines out US 290 and along Hamilton Pool Road, you are getting more houses and businesses and small wastewater treatment plants there."

In 2001, the LCRA built a controversial pipeline to carry surface water drawn from the Colorado River and run through its Uplands treatment plant in Bee Cave. Up to a million gallons a day of water would be pumped to northern Hays County. Save Our Springs Alliance and Save Barton Creek Association sued in federal court to stop the pipeline, claiming harm to the endangered salamanders and birds because of new developments the water pipeline would bring. A judge denied an injunction, despite acknowledging the threat of urbanization posed by the pipeline.

The pipeline was built in a hurry during the 1999–2002 drought over the objections of environmental and other groups. Some groundwater wells were going dry in Sunset Canyon, a subdivision built in the 1980s about four miles east of Dripping Springs off US 290. Hays County declared a drought emergency for the area after 114 residents signed a petition asking for surface water from LCRA. Save Our Springs Alliance attorney Bill Bunch predicted then that county water regulations designed to protect the Edwards Aquifer and the Trinity Aquifer would be eroded: "As soon as you have a central water system, minimum lot size goes down. . . . If you throw in a centralized sewer system, the minimum lot size disappears."

Ten years after the water line was installed, LCRA sold its retail water systems. The West Travis County Public Utility Agency (WTCPUA) was formed to acquire the LCRA system serving the Bee Cave area of Travis County and northern Hays County. An octopus-like network of 260 miles of service lines now is operated by the agency from north of Texas 71 in Bee Cave to south of US 290 in Dripping Springs. An expansion of the WTCPUA's water plant and higher-capacity pump stations is planned to treat up to thirty million gallons a day. Today, new housing developments are building or planned in every direction from Dripping Springs' still-small town center. One of the biggest is Headwaters, named for its location off the north side of US 290 just a couple of miles east of town at the confluence of Little Barton Creek and Barton Creek. With a build-out of one thousand single-family home lots on nearly fourteen hundred acres, the project's first residents moved in in late 2017.

Headwaters for decades was the Hazy Hills Ranch owned by descendants of John C. Townes, the first dean of the University of Texas School of Law. In 2000, the Hill Country Conservancy's George Cofer offered $12 million for the property as watershed conservation land but was turned down. Austin developer (and philanthropist to such organizations as the Salvation Army) Dick Rathgeber tried to develop the property in 2004. He envisioned a low-density project with considerable green space, but he was thwarted by the lingering economic downturn then. Today, the primary developer is Freehold Communities Inc., a Boston-based developer with properties in Florida, Tennessee, North Carolina, and Texas.

Rathgeber, who decades ago developed the Lost Creek subdivision on Barton Creek near Austin and lived there for a while, kept a financial interest in the municipal utility district for the Headwaters land. He says the development will be a good one with plenty of parkland. "I think they're doing a fantastic job," Dick says of the project in general. He also retained three hundred acres on the northern end of the property with creek frontage for a park and gave the Capital Area Council of the Boy Scouts a ninety-nine-year lease on more than sixty acres of that land. The primitive Rathgeber Wilderness Scout Camp has no structures and is accessible only by a rough road. Because campers could be stranded in flood conditions, the camp is seldom used, particularly in rainy seasons. Eventually a better road to the camp will be built, Dick says. He says the development's new residents will be able to walk to the park and the creek on nature trails.

Dick says the developers used "some innovative approaches, particularly in handling storm water. Instead of one big ugly retention pond, they built a series of ponds for about every twenty houses. It separates the houses some." He says there are lots of greenbelts of varying sizes in the project. More houses could have been built under the density and impervious cover regulations. "I guess I'm just kind of an environmentalist at heart and try to make it as low density as I can and still make it work financially."

New subdivisions in the Barton Creek watershed are finding success because of the good school districts, Dick says. But he believes the housing market around Austin is getting "too uncertain and overheated. The merry-go-round is going to stop at some point. It always does. I got in trouble in the late '80s when it all came to a screeching halt, and I'm too old to come back now, so I'm mainly operating in the Rio Grande Valley." He brings a witty close to our conversation: "I like to think of myself as a friend of Barton Creek. I'm going to give that pretty parkland on the creek to Dripping Springs anytime they want the deed. Of course, I'm retaining the name. I figure if people can learn how to spell Zilker, they can spell Rathgeber."

It will take a few years for Headwaters to be built out with a full complement of streets, vehicles, people, and yards that produce the runoff to put any well-designed development to the test. An even larger housing and commercial project called Anarene is planned on both sides of Ranch Road 12 just a mile north of the heart of Dripping Springs. Up to 1,710 housing and commercial units on about that many acres of land are envisioned. The far eastern side of the property will nearly abut Headwaters.

Travis Crow, elected to the Dripping Springs City Council in 2017, is a board member of Dripping Springs Water Supply Corporation, which his grandfather helped found in the 1960s. With four groundwater wells on the south side of town and surface water from LCRA, the company services the old core area of Dripping Springs. We talked about water and sewage issues one afternoon on the outdoor patio of a café on US 290 in Dripping Springs as loud traffic streamed by.

The small town he grew up in now has one of the largest ETJs in the state, a countermove made in the 1980s when Austin was pushing its jurisdiction to the west. "We can't stop growth, we realize that, but we can try to do growth in a smart way. It's always hardball with developers, and we have to draw the line in the sand and tell them what we want. Hopefully, we can come to a reasonable agreement. We're going to be here for the long term, but developers can pack up and leave pretty quickly whenever there's the next recession."

A rare environmental protest movement in northern Hays County took hold in 2016 after Dripping Springs filed for a state permit to expand its sewage treatment facilities, spray more treated sewage effluent on land, and directly discharge up to 995,000 gallons of effluent a day into a tributary of Onion Creek if needed. The city said it is running out of parkland and subdivisions with enough green space to accommodate effluent spraying. About 30 percent of the water going to Barton Springs via the Edwards Aquifer originates in the Onion Creek watershed, which partly adjoins the Barton Creek watershed. Citizen groups, including Protect Our Water and prominent residents on Onion Creek, decried the plan at a public hearing before the Texas Commission on Environmental Quality. The federal Environmental Protection Agency filed an objection to TCEQ's preliminary permit approval but withdrew it in July 2017 after the city revised its plan. The new plan sets a total nitrogen level of six milligrams per liter in the wastewater effluent and includes dechlorination of effluent before any discharge. The city has said it would discharge into the Onion Creek tributary, Walnut Springs Creek, only as a last resort and when there is no flow in Onion Creek a half mile downstream from the discharge site.

A hearing by a TCEQ mediator in May 2018 moved the issue toward a proposed settlement that would reduce the capacity of the treatment plant expansion, irrigate more acreage with treated effluent, and build storage ponds for the effluent. Still, discharges into the creek might be allowed. Several parties objecting to the permit signed onto the settlement, but it didn't go far enough for the veteran battler Bill Bunch of the SOS Alliance. "How much pollution we allow in Onion Creek sets the stage across the Hill Country and other Hill Country streams," he told the *Austin American-Statesman* newspaper. The battle could be decided by administrative law judges. Meanwhile, the vulnerability of Onion Creek took the spotlight when a coalition of groups injected dye into the creek for a study. Traces of the dye soon were detected in seven water wells within a mile. Because the creek recharges Barton Springs even more than Barton Creek, Austinites also took notice.

Wastewater treatment ponds like this one at Rocky Creek are rural subdivision fixtures.

Dripping Springs City Council member Crow wants to keep the issue in perspective. "Which is worse? All this surface pollution from roads and growth going into Onion Creek or the sewage plant discharge?" he asks me without suggesting he has the answer. "I encourage citizens to come talk to us. I honestly feel everyone on the council is trying to do the right thing for the community."

The Onion Creek sewage fight has spurred an ongoing study of direct potable reuse, in which wastewater is treated to drinkable standards with microfiltration, reverse osmosis, and ultraviolet light. Then it is returned to the original water source or the water plant for distribution. (Big Spring has such a system, and other West Texas cities are in the early stages of building reuse systems.) The City of Dripping Springs has asked Dripping Springs Water Supply Corporation to investigate the process, which could cost upward of $9 million and might recycle about five hundred thousand gallons a day of treated wastewater. Crow said of the idea: "I think it is the future for water conservation."

Much time and money have been spent protecting the Onion Creek watershed in recent years. Large tracts of land in the Driftwood and Buda areas now are under conservation easements with the Hill Country Conservancy and other entities. Caves and fissures in and around the creek that funnel water into the aquifer have been enhanced by the Barton Springs Edwards Aquifer Conservation District and the Austin Water Utility Department.

One recharge zone project that took a long time to complete was the cleanout of Crooked Oak Cave. Over years of floods, the cave entrance in the bed of Onion Creek had become clogged with sediment and debris. It no longer created a strong whirlpool on the creek's surface, bringing copious amounts of water into the aquifer. Scientists and workers removed twenty-five feet of sediment (fifty-three cubic yards). It was all done with five-gallon buckets. That's what could fit through the entrance without reinventing what nature had created. And why it took ten years to clear.

David Johns of the city Watershed Protection Department says Austin and Travis County recognized twenty years ago that development of big tracts of land on Barton Creek and its tributaries could be limited by buying them or persuading landowners to donate conservation easements. Hays County has helped protect lands from development in the Onion Creek watershed with past bonds, he says. "But neither Dripping Springs nor Bee Cave has shown much interest in pursuing conservation lands. Perhaps that will change as those communities grow and new residents understand the effects of altering the landscape. Death by a thousand cuts is what we'd have if it were not for the large conservation lands that mitigate what we can't totally control elsewhere on the creeks," he says. "When you change the landscape, you're changing the water ecology as well."

10 GENERATIONS OF CARE

Rancher Henry Brooks and the Puryears Protect Their Lands

Rocking on the cluttered back porch of his house and checking his pastures up the road, Henry Brooks says a lot throughout five hours of the afternoon. With measured thought and astute observations, he talks about the history and care of his land. Henry could be excused at seventy-eight if he just wanted to stay in his rocking chair and reflect on his life in Austin and Dripping Springs. But he keeps moving on this fall day in 2017. We walk to a lush spring and rain catchment tanks downhill of his porch. We drive in his old pickup to another, separate part of his ranch to see where his grandfather kept horses. He tosses out salt blocks for his cows as they crowd around us. He repeatedly climbs from his truck to show me various types of grasses. He points out the prone remnants of cedar trees felled by ax and by chainsaw. He drives to where Barton Creek flows along his property line and talks about how it swelled fivefold after heavy rains last spring.

Back on the porch, we talk about his role in *The Unforeseen*. The 2007 documentary about development battles in Austin features Robert Redford, who learned to swim in Barton Springs Pool. Henry's feet in motion serve as a mystical stand-in for the famed Kentucky poet and environmentalist Wendell Berry. An excerpt from one of Berry's Sabbath series of

Henry Brooks takes porch time at his Dripping Springs ranch that dates to 1905.

poems, "III. Santa Clara Valley," is recited in the film as Henry, face unseen, walks along sidewalks and under highways:

> *I walked that desert of unremitting purpose, remembering*
> *another valley where bodies and events took place and form*
> *not always foreseen by humans, where all the land had not yet*
> *been consumed by intention, or the people by their understanding,*
> *where still there was forgiveness in time, so that whatever*
> *had been destroyed might yet return. Around me as I walked were dogs barking in resentment against the coming of the unforeseen.*
>
> *Copyright 1989 by Wendell Berry. Reprinted by permission of Counterpoint Press.*

Henry owns one of the largest remaining working ranches in the Barton Creek watershed, supporting himself and his son, Harrison. His two tracts of land—a 150-acre homestead on Barton Creek and a 1,900-acre ranch of four pastures and creek tributaries off West Fitzhugh Road north of Dripping Springs—are water-conservation prizes that environmentalists would love to protect forever. Developers envision instead future streets and rooftops if Henry would ever entertain a buyout offer.

"I don't know what to tell you," Henry says when I press him about why he has yet to agree to a conservation easement that could bring in enough cash for himself and his thirty-seven-year-old son to live out their days on their property. An easement would prohibit development in perpetuity. No developers have brought him detailed offers because he tells them not to waste their time and his. What does Henry want? I believe he wants to keep on doing what he does every day, carefully managing his land and telling anyone who will listen what is required to treat it right. Or as he puts it, "What I do is raise vegetation and make decisions about that for my cattle and goats."

By virtue of his decades on the land and his smarts about keeping the soil, grasses, trees, and water healthy, Henry has become something of a Yoda for the Hill Country. Every land-conservation agent I interviewed in Austin told me I should talk to Henry. The same with lifelong Dripping Springs area residents, who grew up respecting him. Ask him anything you want, they said, and he'll tell you as much as he wants to tell you. "Henry is quiet and soft spoken, but he has principles and is very active in taking care of his land," says Travis Crow, a new Dripping Springs City Council member. Travis has known Henry since childhood; his mother was a friend of Henry's late wife, Kay. "I was fed my first green beans by Kay, and Henry gave me my first car, an old Ford Mustang." Henry supports Travis's interest in water issues and making sure growth is done right. Before I visited the Brookses, Travis told me that his political goal is "to do what's best long term for the citizens, the community, and the environment. We should not harm anything—the creeks, the trees, whatever—that's what makes us so beautiful as the Hill Country." Travis sampled it all with a now-legendary hike he and three college friends took down Barton Creek from Dripping Springs to Austin in 1992.

On the Brookses' open back porch full of chairs, Henry shows me old topographical quadrant maps of his two tracts and talks about his family's history on the land in Dripping Springs and in the legal circles of Austin. "These topo maps are just like the ones I used in Vietnam," he says while tracing with a slender finger his property's fence lines and roads, hills and creeks. Henry was a marine lieutenant and patrol leader in the war for four years after he graduated from the University of Texas in 1962. "I was real lucky, and our platoon didn't take any casualties."

He suggests we walk to see a spring that's never been known to cease flowing. "When my grandfather and Judge Robert L. Batts bought this place in 1905, there was a family living out here who used the spring for drinking water. They told them water always came from the spring, even in droughts. Texas Parks & Wildlife has a spring registry, so I registered this one as Mariposa Spring, the name for butterfly in Spanish." First sight of the spring is awesome as it pools in a three-sided rock depression. Brilliant green elephant-ear plants grow from the stream draining out from the spring. We follow the current through the woods to where it passes by a rainwater-collection system. Twin twelve thousand–gallon tanks store water from the rooftop of Henry's house. "We get plenty of water for our needs," he says.

It's feeding time at the ranch, so we move on to a stone-block garage where Henry and Harrison load the bed of a pickup with cattle and goat supplements and a bucket of dry dog food. Then we drive a half mile up Ranch Road 12 to where Henry has been ranching most of his life. As we enter a gate to one of four large pastures, a herd of brood nanny goats, all white bodies and red heads, immediately surrounds our truck. Herding dogs bark behind them but do not come over for a pat. Never do. They're half wild, says Henry of the three dogs that live on the pasture with about two hundred goats. He empties the dogs' bucket into a metal feeder that is protected from the Boer goats by wood fencing. The dogs slip through the wide wood slats to eat. Harrison scoops out from a bucket supplements and a wormer for the goats. Some of the animals soon will be taken to Fredericksburg, the nearest place to sell meat goats.

Next, we drive to a separate pasture with about forty all-black "mama cows" and a couple of young bulls. The cattle, a mix of Angus, Hereford, and Brahman breeds, surround us as Henry lifts thirty-three-pound blocks of protein and salt supplements out of the back of the pickup. He and Harrison toss them amid the cows, who waste no time biting and licking the blocks. Henry examines the low grasses on the

Mariposa Spring flows constantly just steps from Henry Brooks's house.

Harrison Brooks feeds supplements to his father's Boer goatherd.

pasture and laments that he hasn't yet moved the cows to an adjoining pasture where, just over the fence, the grass is about two feet high. "I'll do that soon," he says, adding that cattle should not be allowed to take more than half the volume of grass to ensure its proper regrowth.

As we drive back through the ranch, Henry talks grass and how the land here used to be covered with dense cedar brakes. "After Daddy died in 1983, I got involved with the federal Soil Conservation Service. We had a five-year program that included improvements such as interior fencing to allow pasture rotation and cedar clearing and controlled burns. They did a grass survey before and after. Our grass types changed. Dalton Merz was with the service for thirty years and helped us a lot." The agency is now called the Natural Resources Conservation Service (NRCS).

Henry describes precisely how the cedar brakes were removed. "I didn't burn any of it until long after it was cut. I didn't pile up any trees. I pushed them out of the ground with a tractor so all the roots would come up with them. I let them lay there randomly so long as they weren't near oaks. Over time, the leaves would fall off and lots of grass would come up around the trunks and sticks. After five years of grass growth, we could burn the fields and better control a grass fire instead of a brush fire. A whole lot of cedar sprouts had come up where the trees lay, but the grass fire killed them.

"Before I learned how to do all that, I was just a guy with a tractor piling things up. It's lucky I didn't run over myself. Mr. Merz came out and convinced me there was a better way." He explains that the cut limbs and trunks also help cool the soil and retain moisture otherwise lost to evaporation. "With soil that's too dry, rain comes down and separates the soil into sand and clay and organic matter. When it's separated, the soil isn't productive anymore for grass growth and nutrients aren't available for other plants."

The grasses that grow tall on Henry's land include Indian grass, big and little bluestem, and gamagrass. Unfortunately, there is some King Ranch bluestem, the least beneficial for grazing in Central Texas. It was developed as a hybrid for the historic South Texas ranch decades ago. The Texas Highway Department seeded roadsides with King Ranch bluestem, and it spread across the state. "It's not native and it's not desirable," declares Henry.

He talks—from a lifetime of experience—about low-, mid-, and high-successional grasses. The term applies to how quickly different grasses grow. Low successionals provide fast-growing ground cover first. High successionals like the drought-resistant native gamagrass take longer to grow but are very nutritious. And, he's learned, they are so palatable that overgrazing is a danger. He pulls seeds from the long shoots of various grasses as we walk across his land, and he tells me the name of each plant. Nothing earns his total damnation, even patches of prickly pear cactus and sharp-leafed agarita, a bush that drops berries favored by opossums, birds, and other wildlife. All the growth on his pastures—grasses, trees, and other plants he calls forbs—help create a steady base flow of water into the creeks, he says. Less ground cover and the result from heavy rains is damaging runoff.

We return briefly to the subject of cedars: "Emotionally, I don't think it would be a good idea to get rid of every cedar tree. For one thing, you couldn't because they come up so quickly. For another, we need cedar posts for fencing. But it is a very harmful tree that uses more water than oaks and other deciduous trees that stay dormant all winter. Because cedars never lose their leaves, they are drawing water from the soil all year-round. They're just wicks getting water out of the ground." Henry knows well how the Edwards Aquifer works and its dependence on surface water getting down to it. He concludes my lesson with a smile and a wink toward my book subject of Barton Creek: "That's one manner in which cedar trees tend to diminish spring flow and make it not quite so nice to swim in Barton Springs Pool."

❦

The Brooks' family history resides in Austin courthouses and on Hays County ranches. Henry's grandfather, Victor L. Brooks, was a Travis County district court judge from 1904 to 1907. His father, also named Henry, was a lawyer and the county's district attorney from 1929 to 1931. After his grandfather and Judge Robert Lynn Batts bought about five thousand acres north of Dripping Springs in 1905, the Brooks family often came out from their downtown Austin home to work and enjoy the ranchland. "Judge Batts built the rock house over there, but he never got out here much," says Henry, nodding toward the old house at the end of his porch. "My father did. Judge Batts helped raise Daddy and practiced law with him."

Batts, a former law professor at the University of Texas, was appointed as a judge of the US Fifth Circuit Court of Appeals in 1917. He served only two years before resigning to become general counsel for Gulf Oil Corporation out of state. After returning to Texas in 1923, he was a UT regent for six years and led many building projects for the growing university. Henry, who earned a degree in business administration from UT and never pursued a legal career, told me about his impressive lineage before launching into a story about bending the law.

My grandfather and Judge Batts always hunted after Christmas and would go down to ranches in Mexico for that. On one trip in 1912, they met a young Texan named Thomas Dunn, who was working a herd of cattle on land he owned. Dunn took them hunting with him. They apparently liked him because when sometime later Dunn got in trouble, my grandfather and the judge helped him hide out.

The story goes that Dunn shot and killed a Mexican rancher with a .30-30 rifle in a dispute over water and cattle. Dunn ended up in Austin with a Mexican arrest warrant against him and went to see about his legal rights with attorneys Brooks and Batts. They advised him not to return to Mexico, where they said he'd likely not get a fair trial and die in jail. Then they went a step further. "My grandfather built a little house for him," Henry says. "He lived there pretty much as a recluse. Dunn adopted the alias of Tip May and worked our ranch as foreman. They didn't tell my daddy about his wanted background for a long while. May took Daddy under his wing and taught him all about ropes and horsemanship. He raised horses and mules for us. My mother laughed about Mr. May always being around as her chaperone." Dunn/May also gave Mariposa Spring its name when he was lying low. "Compared to his huge ranch in Mexico, he said this place wasn't big enough to grow anything but butterflies, so he called the spring Mariposa."

Henry resumes my schooling in the ways of nature and perseverance as we continue driving around his nineteen hundred acres of green pastures. (Portions of the original acreage were sold after Judge Batts died.) Fitzhugh Creek and Little Fitzhugh cut ravines through the middle of the land, flowing south to the confluence with Barton Creek. He doesn't draw water from the creeks (wells and rain cisterns provide for his livestock), and he's fenced off the wooded riparian areas so they won't be trampled or polluted by the livestock.

In 2002, the Magellan Pipeline Company, which runs a petroleum pipeline across his property, needed to replace the old piping. Henry made sure he got what he wanted along the more than two miles of right-of-way. New cable and metal-post fencing was put in, with wide gates and cross fencing that allows him to rotate his cows and goats from pasture to pasture. "They didn't do this for anybody else," he says of the deal he got from the company. "The soil types are different out here in different places, so I need to do repeated pasture restoration from one to the other. Back in 1950 they paid my grandmother just sixty dollars for the right-of-way. This time they deserve kudos for going overboard to do something right and followed a plan the conservation service recommended."

I try to change the subject to the future of his land by mentioning that Gary and Jennifer Puryear, who live on 425 acres a few miles east on Rocky Creek, will soon sign on a conservation-easement deal. They get to remain in their house on the land they own, their daughters can build homes on the property if they so desire, and the land will be protected from development forever. One of the four parties financing the deal is the NRCS, which is the same US Department of Agriculture agency that Henry has sought out for advice. He says, yes, he is contacted regularly by land-conservation agents, including Jeff Francell of The Nature Conservancy and Frank Davis of the Hill Country Conservancy. "We've talked in broad, general terms, but we haven't worked out any details. There are a lot of things to consider," he says. Bob Ayres, who manages the nearby Shield Ranch's conservation easement, "told me his family talked about their deal for a long time." Since Henry's wife died in 2001, the Brooks family is down to Henry, a sister who lives in North Carolina, and Harrison, who until recent years traveled frequently to Thailand, Mexico, and Guatemala.

Henry's land is important to the conservancies because of its size, its frontage on creeks, and how well it has been tended by a good conservationist. Location also counts for a lot since the acreage is two miles due west of the Shield Ranch and the Puryears' tract near that. Together with other conservation lands on Barton Creek and tributaries, the Brooks ranch could be a green alternative to a future sea of rooftops and

A lifetime of learning and nurturing results in a lush native landscape.

roads in the middle of the watershed. At this point, the only thing Henry says he's certain about is "I just don't think a housing development is the highest and best use of my land." Henry already is doing many of the water-conservation practices that an easement would require. The natural resources service, for example, did a forage inventory on the land for him. "It wasn't for a conservation easement," he says. "It was just about managing the place." That's exactly what Henry likes to do and apparently intends to keep doing for a good while.

At another stop on the ranch Henry pulls a well-worn photo album from underneath his truck seat. He shows me black-and-white photographs taken at this very spot in 1921 and a few years later. He picks out the faces of his grandfather and Tip May among the scenes of cowboys gathered to dip cattle into water chutes containing a tick-killing pesticide. He talks about the effort it takes to keep the animals healthy: "They are like kids who will eat all of the ice cream but none of the spinach." He makes sure his fields have the most nutritional grasses, not junk food. The one-story, wood-planked house near the cowboys in the photo album remains standing beside us. The son of Henry's longtime friend, the late Thomas Puryear, has lived there with his family for some twenty years. The young couple needed a place to live, so Henry told them they could rent it from him.

I ask about the time he has given over the years to special environmental committees. He was appointed by the US Fish and Wildlife Service to one that considered land-use restrictions in the wake of the Barton Springs salamander being listed as an endangered species. Another committee he served on as a stakeholder proposed a Regional Water Quality Plan in 2005 for the Edwards Aquifer contributing zone in western Travis County and northern Hays County. It's all part of being a good citizen and an informed steward of the land, he says.

When we return to his smaller acreage along Ranch Road 12, he drives across a field with tall grass over the hubcaps and stops just before reaching Barton Creek. A sixty-foot-high cliff lines the opposite bank. Boulders that were part of that cliff many years ago provide jumping platforms when the pooling water is deeper than it is on this day. "We did do a lot of that," Henry says a bit wistfully. He and Harrison compare guesses on how deep and wide the creek was during the last big rainstorm.

A final lesson in letting nature do its thing in and around the creek: "What you really want to do is promote vegetation in the creek. The more of it the better. It's good for the health of the creek. Even the dead limbs and stuff that comes down during floods. See that sycamore tree over there that's got a bunch of debris and is leaning into the water? We're not going to clear that out. We want it to help slow down the next flood that will come along and prevent erosion." I consider picking one of the tall Maximilian sunflowers we wade through on the way back up the bank. Then I think better of messing with anything Henry grows.

Gary and Jennifer Puryear are all smiles as they talk about and absorb the history and beauty of their 425 acres on a deeply cut fork of Rocky Creek. Gary's great-grandfather James Puryear received a land grant for nearly half of the Travis County acreage in 1880. The fading deed, signed by Governor Oran Roberts, hangs in the Puryears' living room. The house where Gary was raised is on the property. Each of the Puryears' four grown daughters lived there at one time or another. Gary and Jennifer reside in a mod-

Jennifer and Gary Puryear's new view from their family acreage is hundreds of rooftops.

est, single-story house built in 1994 near one of the entrances off Crumley Ranch Road. When retirement comes, they'll be happy watching deer and turkeys crisscrossing the fields and the sun setting over the hilltops. Gary is the maintenance manager for Lakeway's nine school campuses. Jennifer sells real estate out of a Westlake Hills office, sometimes to people seeking lake or creek views.

What the Puryears do not want to see are more subdivisions with hundreds of houses closing in on them. They're no longer interested in fending off offers to be bought out. "Some people say we are crazy, that we could get lots of money for this land. I try to explain how it's not mine to sell off. It's my mother's, my late father's, my grandfather's, and his father's," says Gary. "It will be my children's, too." Over the past four years, a plan came together for protecting their land on Rocky Creek, a major tributary of Barton Creek before it flows into Hays County. After hearing how all that unfolded, Gary and I bounce along in his old pickup on the twisting, rocky roads behind his house.

The first gate out encloses a half-dozen goats, just enough to keep down brush on the steep hillsides that can't be mowed. Gary also runs fifteen cows in the fields below, partly for tradition and to get a tax break with an agricultural valuation. As we drive toward the back of the property, we pass the hills where Gary says his daughters could build houses if they choose. He stops in front of a still-solid stone chimney and fireplace that stands like a lone sentry near a grove of majestic live oaks. Gary says the chimney is all that's left from the house where his father was born, so he'll never tear it down.

We walk over to the biggest live oak tree on the ranch. It looks to me like two massive trees, each with towering canopies of branches. When I get closer, I can see that a second trunk, nearly four feet in diameter, is growing out from the main trunk parallel to the ground. It is just a foot or two above the ground for some thirty feet before turning upward with a sprawling crown of its own. Gary says Indians forced it to grow that way. "They would take a young oak tree and tie down a big branch to make it grow sideways. That way they'd have more shade to camp under. We've found artifacts around here, so it likely was a place where they stayed for generations," he says with no doubt about the history story passed down to him.

The fields on both sides of Rocky Creek here are fertile but haven't been planted with crops for decades. Gary's branch starts just beyond his property line to the west, where two small lakes are surrounded by the Deer Creek Ranch subdivision. Most of the houses are on a half acre or more, and some date to the 1960s. Rocky Creek is running half full on this September evening in 2017 despite a near-drought summer. Gary says there are springs in the creek, some he didn't know about until recently, and there is always water moving downstream. We head toward a picnic pavilion built for his family that stands beside a small pond filled by the creek. A rafter of half a dozen turkey hens scurries away from water's edge when we get out of the truck. A large tom lingers but runs after the hens as we walk toward the creek. Leafy sycamores on the banks provide shade for wildlife and human visitors at this pretty spot where the creek takes a sharp turn and tumbles over a small waterfall.

Uphill from here is a campfire spot where the Puryear daughters have long gathered with their friends. They used to get a good view of the stars and little else except the green hills and valley across from the family land. Not so today. A new subdivision named Rocky Creek spreads across those hilltops with curving roads and cul-de-sac arms reaching toward another branch of the creek. The project by Hillwood Communities, headed by Ross Perot Jr. of Dallas, is nearing completion of 395 homes built tightly together on 168 acres. Fortunately, what separates the Puryears from the subdivision is "300 acres of natural habitat," as boasted on an entrance sign. The creek's riparian valley couldn't be built on, but there and on the hills across the creek from the houses five miles of winding trails were created for residents. Rocky Creek

Boulevard was built through the middle of the subdivision to connect Hamilton Pool Road with Crumley Ranch Road.

Gazing at the rooftops visible from his property, Gary says, "That's what our land would look like if we sold out." The Puryears almost did sell. In 2005, a developer approached the couple with a lucrative offer and promises to preserve large areas of green space with multiacreage lots for houses. They signed a contract. But when the developer came back with the actual plan, it had seven hundred houses on two hundred acres. Jennifer remembers: "I said who is going to want to come out here for that? I'm in real estate, and I'm happy for things to develop, but not in a crazy way." They tore up the contract.

I tell Gary what Frank Davis, director of land conservation for the Hill Country Conservancy, had recently told me: "I'm always fascinated by people who are drawn out to the country to live in these developments. You're staring into your neighbors' backyards with maybe a view of the hills in the distance. In these dense developments, you're living an urban lifestyle without all the amenities of the city and having a long commute."

Yet I also recognize another view, one expressed by developer Jim Meredith. He expects construction to start in early 2019 on 664 houses planned for his Provence development up Hamilton Road from the entrance to the Rocky Creek subdivision. I visit with him in his office as bulldozers outside are clearing the land. Why are people drawn to these new subdivisions in the country, I ask him. "They're looking for a place to raise their kids with good schools," he says. "These are working people who can't get into Westlake Hills for less than a million bucks for houses. We have the Bee Cave mall, office buildings, hotels, H-E-B, Home Depot. They're looking for affordability and those infrastructures of Bee Cave and Lakeway. This isn't the country anymore."

Jim says that "one hundred percent of what I'm doing out here is according to Travis County ordinances and without variances. When we did mediation with a handful of neighbors, they started getting into land use and saying we had to do this and do that. I don't think they were truly concerned about the environment as much as protecting their own million-dollar real estate values as opposed to our houses that will be in the $400,000 to $650,000 range. I told them I would work with them on four water-filtration ponds and downstream protection, but they were all about lot size. As a result of the settlement, we're going to add some trees, filtration traps, and setback buffers from Little Barton Creek and tributaries." He says landowners who want to get conservation easements "absolutely have that right, but I'm also for land entitlement rights as a developer."

A couple of miles to the south, Gary Puryear finishes driving me around his property with the sun setting behind us. I recognize an old gray barn ahead of us across Crumley Ranch Road. It's the back entrance to the Shield Ranch, the largest conservation land on Barton Creek—sixteen times the size of the Puryears' property. The horizon of fields and hilltops on the ranch is all shades of green. The Puryears had never met Bob Ayres, who manages the ranch for his family but lives in Austin. They knew the ranch was under a conservation easement but did not know how such an arrangement worked.

About four years ago, John Hatchett, who lives off Hamilton Pool Road and is a longtime friend of Gary's, suggested the couple look into such an easement to protect their property. Hatchett at the time was considering developing his own land as part of Jim Meredith's Provence project. That might still happen, doubling the size of Provence, if permits for more water can be acquired. "John is very conscientious about the environment and is still helping us understand our easement," says Gary. Then he laughs and says, "Well, maybe he's just eliminating us from competition with his own project."

A conservation easement forever protects the Puryear land from subdivisions like Rocky Creek next door.

Hatchett introduced the Puryears to Frank Davis of the Hill Country Conservancy. Then Ayres invited the Puryears to see the Shield Ranch and met with them for two hours to explain the various options possible under conservation easements. "Days later we started getting calls from Travis County officials and other parties that could help us with an easement on the land," says Gary. He took the idea to his eighty-five-year-old mother and sole owner of most of the land, Alice Puryear Perkins. "She said she thought my dad would have liked this more than selling the land and cutting it up and turning it into something else. Dad loved this place and all his history was here. This way our kids and grandkids will be able to enjoy it, too."

The plan Davis put together is a conservation easement that allows the family to continue owning the property and living there for generations. Partners in the deal are the NRCS, Travis County, Texas Parks & Wildlife Department, and the Hill Country Conservancy. NRCS and Travis County are each paying about half the money the Puryears will receive for giving up development rights on their land in perpetuity. NRCS is using funds dedicated to protecting the water and ecological resources of ranchlands from development. The county is drawing from conservation-easement bonds approved by voters in 2011. Texas Parks & Wildlife has paid transaction costs for such things as surveys and appraisals.

The Puryears will manage the land's water, vegetation, wildlife, and animal stock with the assistance and expertise of the easement partners. Gary is pleased the easement allows him to continue the traditions of running a small cattle herd and hunting deer. (He said surrounding development in recent years has pushed too many deer onto his land.) An inventory of trees, grasses, and birds on the property has already been done by the conservancy to draw up vegetation- and wildlife-management plans.

To give their daughters a future stake in the land, the Puryears' easement stipulates that houses can be built on the property for them in addition to the house where their one daughter lives now. Each house would be on a specified, separate five-acre tract away from Rocky Creek and with limits on impervious cover. Gary and Jennifer plan to remain in their house on a three-acre plot bought from his mother years ago. The bottom line for Gary is, "We want the community to be proud of our project here. That's our goal."

Frank Davis says, "The Puryears are fortunately nestled down in a valley with Rocky Creek flowing through it. That will ensure clean water going onto the Shield property across the road and eventually into Barton Creek. That's the type of conservation easement we like to see strategically. It's the most urgent work we do in a watershed if we can afford it or find a charitable landowner."

In the meantime, the Puryears try to accept what's around them and still coming. "We are now the great view for the Rocky Creek subdivision," Jennifer says with resignation. She is happy that new nearby restaurants, distilleries, breweries, and wineries give her and Gary more options for eating and drinking. Wedding venues have provided employment for two of their daughters. "Those businesses are sort of like farms and try to have a low impact. But the traffic is terrible, and everyone needs to slow down on our narrow roads. All our girls have had wrecks."

Gary sees an occasional danger now from the converged branch waters of Rocky Creek that pass under a low-water crossing bridge on Crumley Ranch Road. "I've only seen water over there three times in my life," he says. "Twice it happened in 2016 with water chest high after flooding rains. Unbelievable. I tell my kids to be careful driving over there. Everything has changed with all the rooftops, yards, and streets draining down toward the creek." What won't change under the protection of a conservation easement is the 425 acres the Puryears call their forever home.

11 CONSERVING HISTORY

Reviewing an Easement Where an 1800s Pioneer Era Ended

Doug Doerr arrives for an appointment at his historic getaway cabin on a too-warm-for-November morning. The annual conservation-easement review for his 143 acres of Hill Country grassland and old-growth oaks finally fits into his busy IT consulting schedule. This is one of the first places I visited nearly two years earlier when my wife and I would drive the narrow Hays County roads in search of Barton Creek's beginnings. We gradually became emboldened enough on weekend afternoons to stop at places where someone could be spotted outside. I'd come down the gravel driveways and blurt out my mission: I'm writing a book about Barton Creek, and I'd like to ask you about your piece of heaven. Or something like that.

When I introduced myself to Doug in front of his very old cabin and a new garage under construction, he welcomed my questions. He spent his youth in San Marcos and appreciated the springs of the Blanco and San Marcos Rivers. Those memories played into his 2008 decision to buy property with a mile of Barton Creek winding through the middle. He and his wife, Kiff; their son; daughter; and friends have since spent countless days swimming in and sitting beside the creek. I didn't know that a conservation easement came with the land or that his property once was encompassed by a thirteen hundred–acre ranch whose owner chose the protective covenant in perpetuity. Doug, who lives in Austin, invited me to return

Doug Doerr plans to restore this storied 1800s cabin and build an adjoining house.

for a tour and a hike along the creek. He warned me that I should take care not to rattle up a diamondback, which recently happened to his wife in her garden near the cabin. "Just keep your eyes open where you're stepping," he said.

When I return with my hiking buddy, Doug takes us on his four-wheeler to where Barton Creek runs beside a soaring cliff. A high-up section of that limestone, with one piece about the size of a small car, slid into the creek after a heavy rain just weeks before my visit. Doug says it's exciting to see the results of a natural erosion event that changes the landscape. And, he notes, a new hole for swimming probably will form near the boulder. He shows us another area of the creek where wild hogs have uprooted grasses and seedlings, wallowing in the banks and destroying sapling trees. They're invasive and multiply rapidly, so Doug hunts them every chance he gets.

We cross the creek on an old ranch road and head up into the hills for views of the valley that roughly parallels McGregor Lane. I can see the tree line along the banks of Barton Creek where, on a neighbor's property, the creek flows under Martin Road about two miles east of its source. The former pastures—no cattle, goats, or horses since Doug bought the land—hug the creek with pretty, swaying mixes of bluestem and Indian grass. Giant oaks dot the fields. He points out a sprawling one behind the cabin where his kids, now in college, built a treehouse.

Doug stops his four-wheeler at the back fence of his property and says my friend and I can hike down from here to pick up the creek back to his place. The steep, rocky road we follow is getting squeezed into oblivion by big cedars. It is a shaded and incredibly quiet route that likely saw creaking wagons in the 1800s. An hour or so walk downhill and along the creek brings us back to the cabin, where Doug is out back tinkering with some grass-shredding equipment. He takes us around to the front to show off what his family has picked up around the property. The porch railing top is lined with the skeletal remains of deer, reptiles, and small mammals. Fossils and rocks of all shapes, sizes, and ages lie between the bones.

This small limestone-block house was built in the "dogtrot" style of Texas pioneers, with an open breezeway between two living areas. Over the years before the Doerrs bought the property, the cabin was remodeled to fill in the open space with a hallway and add a kitchen and bathroom to the back. A cozy living room with a fireplace and a fourteen-foot-ceiling is on one side of the hallway. A bedroom and another fireplace are on the other. Doerr has done some restoration and repairs, but he says he'd like to do much more to return the structure to its original state.

The cabin is part of a difficult period in Hays County history, built in 1868 according to county deed records Doerr has seen. The owner was Lorenzo D. Moore, one of the area's earliest Anglo settlers and a Hays County commissioner. Moore's grave is across the road in a small private cemetery, and his headstone records the violent confrontation that took his life.

Early on a springtime Sunday morning, Lorenzo Daw Moore stepped out of his cozy stone cabin to get one of his horses ready for a trip to San Marcos. He'd likely find the mare and her foal in the pasture between his house and Barton Creek. The thirty-mile ride by buggy from his farm northwest of Dripping Springs was a chore but one he had signed onto as a member of the Hays County Commissioners Court. He would spend the night down at the county seat and then attend the monthly court meeting the next day before heading back home to his wife, Mary; their four children; and his mother, Polly.

Moore had served on the court for two years and before that had been a county surveyor. He was involved in creating and maintaining the Austin to Fredericksburg road where it crossed Hays County. But on this fine morning of May 19, 1872, the first thing on his mind was where to find his horse.

Lorenzo D. Moore, a Hays County commissioner, lived in the cabin until 1872. (Courtesy of Jean Quist Sellstrom family)

Another member of the court and a countryside neighbor, Pleasant Duke Alexander, planned to travel to San Marcos with Moore. Alexander and family lived a few miles down Barton Creek in a large five-room house. The settler from Tennessee had prospered on Colorado River land in Bastrop County before moving his family to Hays County in 1855. Alexander was appointed county judge in 1867 and oversaw completion of a new courthouse building.

The fifty-five-year-old Moore was an Illinois native who had been a wheelwright in Austin before moving to upper Barton Creek with his family. Moore's brother Enoch was county attorney and postmaster and had a business selling properties in San Marcos. After calling for his mare and checking the pasture without finding her, Lorenzo Moore decided he'd better walk up the creek with his dog. He knew Indians frequented the area, but most of them were friendly enough and just wanted to trade with the settlers. Moore's mother, Polly, remembered with horror more dangerous times in rural Illinois. In 1814, she survived the Wood River Massacre by Indians there that left seven members of her extended family dead, including two of her young sons. Her son Lorenzo was born three years later, and she eventually moved to Texas to live with his family.

What Moore came upon while searching for his mare was a small band of Comanches, the nomadic and reservation-resistant horsemen who mostly had been driven to the west and north of Central Texas by 1872. They were encamped a short distance from his house, roasting his foal for food. Whatever protests the unarmed Moore might have mustered, he was shot in the back by one arrow and two others in his head. The Indians left with his mare, and his dog led neighbors to Moore's body. Moore may have been the last person in Hays County killed by Indians, according to several accounts.

The Hays County Commissioners Court passed a resolution a few weeks later noting that their "esteemed brother" was "brutally murdered near his house in the county by a band of savages." The commissioners resolved "that by his sudden death it forcibly reminds us of the uncertainty of life" and that "the county has lost an efficient officer and honest and upright citizen." Today, in a small family cemetery surrounded by woods just a quarter-mile from the Moore cabin, his gravestone simply states:

L. D. MOORE
KILLED BY INDIANS
1817–1872

Frank Davis is visiting the Doerrs' historic cabin in late 2017 for the Hill Country Conservancy's annual

A marker in a nearby cemetery records Moore's epitaph: "KILLED BY INDIANS."

conservation-easement review with the present landowner. He has brought a printed checklist to note how the property has been cared for since the last review. The director of land conservation for the conservancy will go through the easement requirements with Doug, asking questions and offering advice. The three of us sit in the western-styled living room of the cabin. I'm eager to hear what happens during the review.

Among the questions on Frank's checklist: Any new structures built? Is brush cover being maintained? Any agricultural use (grazing, haying, or farming)? Have synthetic fertilizers or pesticides been employed? Noticed any new invasive plants or animals? Among the water questions: Have creeks and riparian areas been significantly impacted by livestock or erosion? Any alteration, depletion, or extraction of surface water or natural water courses? New wells, ponds, or stock tanks? Any water pollution due to on-site or off-site activities? Any changes to historic structures or archaeological sites on the land?

None of Doug's answers appear to raise serious issues. They talk about problems such as prickly pear cactus spreading in the fields. Frank recommends PastureGard as a safe herbicide for the cactus, but he says some prickly pear should be retained as "a native, important part of the habitat. It provides cover for quail and dove. But, yes, it can be invasive."

They discuss current rainfall problems with the first half of the year mostly wet and the second half dry. Barton Creek across Doug's land is mostly without water this November. Doug says he is filling a trough from his well for some of the wildlife around the cabin. Several wild turkeys ran across the field outside when I arrived. Frank suggests the alternative of a rainwater-collection tank with a one hundred–square-foot catchment roof that might provide enough water for the critters.

Doug spends some weekends in the winter months shredding the native grass varieties that grow well in his fertile, floodplain pastures. Each pasture is cut just once a year. Plowing can help growth in a few specific areas, says Frank. He adds that he'll send Doug some of the latest research information about that practice. When the checklist question about riparian erosion comes up, Doug says he has a problem in one place. He and Frank decide to take a walk to the site to look at what's happening. Near the family swimming hole, one bank of Barton Creek has seriously eroded into the pasture above, endangering a large cedar elm. They discuss the possibility of building a wood retaining wall backfilled with rocks and soil to protect the tree's roots. As we return to the cabin along an expansive mix of grasses, bushes, and trees, Frank tells me, "Whatever Doug is doing to manage this area, he's doing a great job."

When we're inside again, Doug brings out prelimi-

Conservancy land director Frank Davis surveys the owner's work with grasses.

nary plans drawn for building a large house on the property. The easement allows just one residence, so the idea is to encompass the existing stone cabin on three sides with the new house and tie it all into the garage already built next door. I can hear in Doug's voice his excitement about the cabin-restoration part of the project. He says he'll tear out the modern wallboards, ceiling, and flooring to get down to whatever the cabin looked like when it was built in the 1800s. "We've got to get through all this mess added on over the years to know what we've got here. I have no idea what the original foundation was like, and I want to understand how pier-and-beam construction was done back when the Moores lived here."

Doug's property and many more acres above this valley of Barton Creek were once owned by Jack Bleakley, a University of Texas geology graduate from Boerne and San Antonio. He made a fortune in natural gas production in the 1950s and 1960s, settled in San Angelo, and often returned to the Hill Country he loved. I talked briefly on the phone to Bleakley in 2016, when he was ninety-four years old, about six months before he died. He said he bought the land—1,960 acres for $65,000—in 1956 from a San Antonio Episcopal minister and his wife. Visits to his Far Hills Ranch, where Bleakley ran cattle, were more frequent once he built a landing strip for the small plane he flew. It was a favorite part of his long life, he told me. His daughter and son and their grandparents enjoyed living on the land for months at a time, staying in the Moore cabin and in other houses on the ranch. "I built a small dam on Barton Creek so we could have a place to swim," he said. "There was an old Indian camp up on the hill above the creek, and that's where I found a lot of arrowheads."

In 1982, Bleakley was interviewed by *Austin American-Statesman* reporter Pete Szilagyi. The headline read "Spring's Owner Cares for Friends Downstream." The article continued: "Headwaters might be too dramatic to describe the diminutive pool of cool, clear spring water that rises on the edge of Jack Bleakley's Hays County ranch." Standing near a seep where

CONSERVING HISTORY

he said the ground is wet year-round, the geologist described the fault lines that bring water to the surface. He showed Szilagyi a thirty-foot-deep lake he had built behind a dam on Schoolhouse Hollow so he could release water slowly down to Barton Creek. "As a geologist, I understand a lot more about hydrology and understand how the water percolates through the soil. But even if I hadn't had the training, I still would have taken the conservation measures. You have to watch out for what's downstream."

What once was Far Hills Ranch could be considered part of the creek's headwaters, but it is itself downstream of other small tributaries and the westernmost beginnings of Barton Creek. In the spring of 2017, I followed the narrowing creek by road and by foot with topographical maps to a pasture surrounded on three sides by steep hills. A couple of miles from the Bleakley ranch, I found the spot where Barton Creek first forms a continuing stream.

In May 2000, the Bleakley family put thirteen hundred acres of their land under a conservation easement held by The Nature Conservancy. At that time, the tract was the second-largest such protected acreage in the Barton Creek watershed. Only the Shield Ranch's easement near Bee Cave two years earlier surpassed it. Jeff Francell, director of land protection for the conservancy's Austin office, remembers when he was hired in 1998:

> The idea was that I would go figure out all the landowners upstream of the Barton Creek Habitat Preserve and try to get conservation easements from them. The first thing we did was put together an ownership map. That's how I figured out the Bleakleys had the biggest chunk of land near the headwaters for the watershed.
>
> Jack Bleakley approached me and said he was getting old and was going to sell it, but he really would like to see it conserved. I spent a lot of time with him. We bought the ranch with no public money involved and sold it with the right to be divided into different pieces. Many of those pieces now have houses on them, but we conserved that thousand-plus acres of land. From a watershed standpoint, the amount of development that has occurred out there is not having any bad impact on Barton Creek. It is still a functioning landscape. Having this preserve mitigates erosion and some of the pollution from any new development in the area.

Family members retained some of the Far Hills ranchland, but the much larger protected acreage now is divided among five owners. All the properties keep in perpetuity the conservation easement bought by The Nature Conservancy and assigned later to the Hill Country Conservancy for oversight. Hill Country's Frank Davis is an eloquent voice for the big picture of such conservation lands in Texas:

> They are a way for us to protect the land, the water, the wildlife, the scenic views, the heritage of our state. Dealing with government agencies is important in these deals, but the myth that we're seeking to somehow transfer this property to any government entity is nonsense. The goal is to have a forever deal between the private landowner and us as a private nonprofit trust. Most of the landowners who do these deals with us are already conservation minded. They understand our role and their ownership. These people commonly say their land is near and dear to them, but they don't know what will happen with it when they're gone because their children don't want to or can't move back here. They don't want their land to become a commodity for a developer.
>
> It's easy to bemoan all the development and changes going on, but it is also worth celebrating that we can float in peace in these natural places. It's a novel time in history that we have full bellies and are not worried about where our next meal is coming from or if there will be an Indian raid. We own the land outright and can enjoy it. That hasn't happened before in history here. Not to be too dismal, but prices are so high along Barton Creek and most of the large parcels

are spoken for, so we have to move farther west where there isn't so much development potential and landowners are more charitable toward us.

Jack Bleakley's daughter, Anne Shahan, brings up fond memories of her time on the family's Far Hills Ranch when I call her in San Angelo. "I loved what we called the little house. My brother and I lived there for many of our formative years with my parents," she says of the Moore cabin on Barton Creek. Anne remembers the creek's big holes of water and turns and twists. "We played in those holes and in the waterfalls. Catfish and perch hid out under the rock shelves. A lot of mornings we'd catch a fish for breakfast before the school bus came. It was a great place to grow up—wonderful."

Although Anne's permanent home is in San Angelo, she spent several months of every year on the ranch in the 1960s and 1970s. She and her brother, Mark Bleakley, attended school some years in Dripping Springs. Her grandparents lived up the hill from the cabin. "My mother [Marian Kingsbery Bleakley] was raised in Austin. She swam in Barton Springs and Barton Creek as a kid. Barton Creek and the Hill Country was important to my father as well when he went to the University of Texas, which was interrupted by World War II."

The family's long history with the area and its essential water sources was a big factor in the decision to put a conservation easement on most of the ranch in 2000. Shahan says she and her brother were involved in discussions about the easement that would be attached to the property forever. "Of course, it was my father and mother's decision, but we were brought to the table. Since we were raised there, we loved the place very, very much, and we're still incredibly sentimental about it." She said the family knew what it meant to put an easement on the ranch because they had been approached earlier about doing so with another ranch her parents owned in the Big Bend area:

We said no to that, but let's talk about our ranch in Dripping Springs. We hated seeing what was going on with all the Austin growth. Because our ranch was on Barton Creek and because things were changing so rapidly with regulations coming out of Austin about what you could and couldn't do with your land, some of them pretty random, it made sense for us. But it was difficult because we weren't abusers of the land. We knew what we had, and we treasured it. We did not want to get regulated by people telling us what we could and couldn't do, but we also did not want the land to go to development when it meant so much not only to us but to the people of the Hill Country and in Austin.

With Anne's father well into his seventies in the late 1990s, there also was the issue that estate taxes might force the ranch to be sold. "That had a lot to do with us putting it into a conservation easement and making sure it was preserved," she says. Today, she owns 240 acres of the original ranch. There is no house on the property, but from San Angelo she manages to keep an eye on what is happening in the rural neighborhood. The news is not good.

Two other former ranchlands turned into subdivisions have begun building along US 290 between Bell Springs Road and McGregor Lane. Developers embraced the idea of life in the country by naming them Bunker Ranch (165 homesites) and Arrowhead Ranch (380 homesites). The latter reaches down to Onion Creek and advertises, "The outstanding highway access makes the 20-mile commute to downtown Austin a breeze." Perhaps that breeze is possible when traffic slows after midnight.

At the northwest corner of McGregor and 290, a 680-acre spread was John Farley's ranch when the Bleakleys had their place just up McGregor. That property now is slated for development of more than nine hundred houses. Shahan came to Austin in August 2017 for a Dripping Springs City Council meeting to consider preliminary approval of the first two phases

A limestone bluff tumbled down to create a new rocks feature in Barton Creek on Doug Doerr's land.

of the plan. She said previous developers tried to put subdivisions there, but it never happened. This time the Westwood subdivision, owned by the California-based development company SunCal, appears on its way to a construction start before long.

Plat designs for the first two phases of the development won preliminary approval at the council meeting. The city earlier had brought the land into its extraterritorial jurisdiction and rezoned it from agriculture use to a Planned Development District. Phases 1 and 2 of the Westwood subdivision will bring some six hundred houses. Phases 3 and 4 will add about three hundred more houses. The project also includes the developer's contribution for road improvements, some for access to the subdivision. The council said it is satisfied the development follows the Dripping Springs Conservation Design Ordinance, enacted in 2014.

Anne says the first two phases are in the Onion Creek watershed, and the second two—conceptual at this point, according to the council—are on hillsides in the Barton Creek watershed. "It's a shame. What people want to move to the Hill Country for won't still be there if we let greed run rampant. Now that they're going to mess up the headwaters, who knows what's going to happen?"

12 🌿 THE BEGINNING

Ralph Roy Breed's Pasture Trickle and a Farm for Cheesemaking

It begins here as a cow-pasture trickle on 250 acres of lush grass and uncrowded oaks. Barton Creek's source, some fifty twisting waterway miles from where the creek ends at the Colorado River, forms on Roy Ralph Breed's land northwest of Dripping Springs. A tiny stream takes shape from squishy soil under the grass. Everything on three sides of the horizon is a ridge or a hill, including peaks more than fifteen hundred feet in elevation. Rains and seeps bring water down to Roy Ralph's land from a neighbor's large, gently sloping and uncut field behind his fenced pasture. A foot-deep ditch on his side of the fence is the start of Barton Creek.

The stream is just wide enough for my legs to stretch across in an easy leap. The most remarkable nearby feature is a cottonwood tree with a trunk four feet in diameter. Well-nourished, obviously. No springs are visible here, though Roy Ralph tells me there is a spring where he had a tank dug for his cattle. That was a few years after he bought the acreage in 1965. He paid $100 an acre for 130 acres then and added more in later years. The tank is a pretty tear-drop-shaped pond with a short, rickety wood fishing pier poking into the water. The pier is too far gone for us to walk out, and the catfish he used to stock in the tank are gone, too. He said the tank has dried up

Below steep hills, Barton Creek starts a fifty-mile journey to its end in Austin.

during severe droughts, but it usually has plenty of water for his twenty-five head of cattle.

Downstream from the tank, brimming from April's rains in 2017, Barton Creek flows east as a tiny current. It crosses under Martin Road through a single, two-foot-wide culvert. It doesn't feel like a substantial creek until it leaves another of Roy Ralph's pastures and is joined by a small tributary stream from the south. As it runs parallel to Martin Road, new homes and old farmsteads get a real creek out back, lined by tree canopies and pooling into occasional swimming holes.

As Barton Creek meanders toward Travis County, it is fed by dozens of tributaries and springs in its watershed of 109 square miles. The watershed mostly is in the contributing zone of the Edwards Aquifer, but when the creek gets just a few miles from the Colorado River, it crosses over the aquifer's critical recharge zone. Finally, just before the creek ends, springs bring up refreshing water from the aquifer to fill Barton Springs Pool.

"I always knew Barton Creek was here, but we'd go into Austin to swim with our kids," says Roy Ralph, who uses the two given names to distinguish himself from his late father, Roy. The Breed family tree has branches growing all over the far end of Barton Creek. "I remember Deep Eddy Pool as cold and Barton Springs as a bit warmer." (Deep Eddy, on the opposite shore of the Colorado River from Zilker Park, is filled daily from an old hand-dug well with water ranging from sixty-five to seventy-five degrees. Barton Springs Pool, fed by springs, averages sixty-eight to seventy degrees.)

Tall and rangy in his mid-seventies, Roy Ralph is content to manage his cattle on the pasture with the creek source and fifty goats he keeps on another part of his land across Martin Road. "It's enough," he says as we climb into his pickup to drive a short distance to the creek. Rain clouds on a cool spring day threaten to unload on us, and he is prepared with a gimme cap and a denim jacket. We had met at the well-worn, cedar-shingled house where he and his wife, Connie, mostly spend weekends. They used to live in the small house full-time, but Breed tired of the drive to the IBM plant in north Austin where he worked in security and

Roy Ralph Breed put a livestock and fishing tank at a spring site on the creek in 1965.

fire prevention, so they bought a house near his job and retired there. It's obvious, though, that he prefers the country life over the city one. Connie grew up in Luckenbach fifty miles east and keeps sheep out there on her land, which still has a house without electricity.

The past is not that far gone around this area for the Breeds. Roy Ralph remembers his father going out into pastures on horseback to make telephone line repairs after storms took down their service. "He did what was needed to make sure we had our phone working," the son tells me.

An old stacked rock wall separates the Breeds' house from their barn. Cattle guards across Martin Road at each end of the property keep the cows confined. I had driven this road before and knew to slow down to let cows move out of the way. Roy Ralph's goats are fenced in farther down the road because—his tone indicating not everyone knows this fact—"goats will just jump over a cattle guard."

We drive a short distance from the house, and he turns his truck into a grassy field. He weaves between mature trees and beyond his tank to the spot where Barton Creek begins. It is obvious from the steep, sandy banks of the little waterway that, at times, the water runs fast here. On this day, it is barely moving but still deep enough that water would come over our boot tops if we step into it instead of jumping over it.

Roy Ralph talks about his efforts to help nature along here. He has taken out most of the cedar trees so they don't crowd out the oaks. He shoots a deer occasionally to keep that population in check. He doesn't let his goats graze on this part of his land because they would eat everything. He's proud that his tank was built right and has lasted for decades. The idea that Barton Creek starts on his property and is appreciated many miles away pleases him. But mostly he's happy when the tank fills from rainfall and the spring at the bottom. I ask him later if he'd allow a City of Austin biologist to dive in his tank in a long-shot search for salamanders. "That's not something I'd be interested in," he says flatly.

On the spring day of our visit, his land won't get more than a few sprinkles from the dark skies. After my friend Alberto shoots photos of the creek from

A trickle becomes Barton Creek as it crosses Breed's ranch in northwestern Hays County.

every angle, I ask Roy Ralph if we can see more of his neighborhood. He had told me the house he grew up in was just a half mile down Martin Road, so we head that way. It is a nicely kept place with a limestone exterior, metal roof, and an inviting front porch. His brother Terry Breed lives there. Although Roy Ralph lived in this house until he left home, what holds the most vivid memory for him lies across the road from the house. Roy Ralph's father was born nearby on McGregor Lane. His sister lives a quarter mile farther down Martin on a private road she had the county name Roy Breed Road. His cousin Truman and two of Truman's siblings have acreage on West Fitzhugh Road. Another cousin, Caroline Breed Gully, lives off US 290 west of Dripping Springs.

Like many of his relatives, Roy Ralph worries that "they're building too much out here. See that ridge over there?" he says pointing southeast from his house. "That's going to be covered with 912 houses planned from there to the corner of McGregor and 290. I know there's always someone wanting to make changes, but...." His voice trails off. "I can smell already what's coming up from my neighbors' septic tanks after a heavy rain," he says.

Roy Ralph's son, Glenn, is a professor in Florida, but he hopes his daughter, Rhonda, who lives in Karnes City, will take on the land after he and his wife pass. "She was always a big help to me on the ranch. She's a real outdoor lady." The acre-size garden behind his house on Martin Road will also need tending. It is rich with okra, tomatoes, cantaloupe, and cousa, a round green squash he likes a lot. "We take that cousa, mash up the meat with some brown sugar, and fry it. It's wonderful. And the cantaloupes grow like crazy. I took eighty of them to the dance hall in Dripping Springs and gave them to everyone."

The new neighbors around his land have two things to learn, Roy Ralph maintains. One is the importance and, to him, the sanctity of the fences that keep in his cattle and goats. "These folks moved in and had a worker take down my fence in a spot between us. I went over and said, 'What are you doing?' They said it didn't look good, and they would build it back. I told them, 'No, I'll do it.' That made me two-thirds mad." He says his second big concern is the dogs that come with new neighbors and are permitted to run free in the country. "Half my kid goats get killed by dogs. Hays County has a leash law, I tell them. Over and over, one lady claimed her dogs never left her property even though I saw them here. I finally told her if they're on my property, they're dead."

Still, Roy Ralph loves coming out to where so many memories in his life were made. As we're leaving his boyhood home, he points across the road to a small pile of stone rubble and a block of rough concrete with three steps. That was his family's first house. "Some things stick with you forever. I was five on a January day when my father got up in the morning and turned on our coal-oil stove. It exploded. We all got out—my mom and dad and older sister and me. Everything burned up, including my new tricycle. The only things that were saved were two family quilts." Back at his place, he points to the rusting hulk of his '48 Chevy coupe that sits far out in a field on the opposite side of his house from the creek source. "My wife used it as a deer blind for a while. I just like to look at it."

Goats are an important but different kind of asset for another family near where Barton Creek begins. A couple of miles east on Martin Road from Roy Ralph Breed's house, Amelia Sweethardt and her three sisters have operated their Pure Luck Farm and Dairy since their mother Sara Sweetser first tilled the soil above the creek in 1979. While Breed's goats are auctioned off for meat, Pure Luck's herd of one hundred Nubian and Alpine goats produce sweet, fresh milk to make goat cheese. I had asked Breed if he knew the late Sweetser. "Yes, I visited there and she came over here to my place. Nice lady," he said. Did he ever try her goat cheese? "No, sir, it's just not for me," he said. Pure

Luck's cheese has been a big seller for years at outlets in Austin, including Wheatsville Co-op, Whole Foods, Central Market, and some farmers' markets. The cheeses have won several national awards, including a 2017 award by the American Cheese Society for the feta.

Gitana and Amelia were four and two when their mother created the Pure Luck organic farm, growing herbs, vegetables, melons, and flowers on eleven acres where an old house sat in front of former tomato fields. The terraced land slopes down to a four hundred–foot stretch of Barton Creek. Today, the fields produce herbs—spearmint, dill, oregano, thyme, and rosemary—sold in bulk to Central Market. The goatherd and dairy operation that Sweetser and her husband, Denny Bolton, started in 1995 is across the road on another fifty acres that includes family houses. Amelia and Gitana Sweethardt and their younger stepsisters, Claire and Hope Bolton, all live on the property and help produce and market the Pure Luck products.

The creek is where everyone gets to cool off on hot days between morning and afternoon milkings and tending the herb crops. "We'd play forever and ever

Amelia Sweethardt's herd awaits milking at Pure Luck Dairy across from Barton Creek.

in the little falls and pools of water there. Sometimes we'd walk in the creek all the way to the road bridge. We even tried ice skating on the creek in the winter, but that wasn't too successful," says Amelia.

From her house, Amelia and I walk to the dairy barn through a series of fences separating yard chickens, turkeys, and dogs from the goats. The does, bucks, and kids each have their own areas. It's late afternoon and seventy-some udders are full, so the adult females cluster around the ramp into the milking room. They literally get in line so ten at a time can stand with heads in a feed trough and teats hooked into suction cups and vacuum hoses. The machinery delivers an average sixty gallons a day of raw milk to stainless-steel vats to await the cheese-making process. Together with the repeated cleaning of equipment and teats, the milking alone takes a couple of hours twice a day. Another four days of work goes into making Pure Luck's cheeses: pasteurizing the milk, adding lactic acid to form curds, draining the curds, salting and more draining, and cutting and packing the feta, chevre, and soft-ripened blue varieties into small plastic tubs.

Despite the dairy's location just eight miles west of Dripping Springs' town center, the feeling here is all country, with the farm surrounded by woods and few neighbors. Amelia says coyotes lurk nearby, but the families' dogs keep them from attacking the goats. As we walk across the road to the herb fields and Barton Creek, she tells me of her plans to open a retail cheese shop in a small house moved onto the property from Austin. There are now enough visitors coming out this way to wedding venues, wineries, and distilleries to support that kind of business, she believes. Also, Dripping Springs is growing rapidly, pushing west along US 290 with new housing subdivisions in the city's ETJ.

Amelia is not a fan of that kind of development and the amount of traffic it will bring, but she is resigned to the inevitable. She attended a Dripping Springs City Council meeting in 2017 with several neighbors who also were concerned about the most recent big subdivision planned for the northwest corner of McGregor Lane and US 290. The Westwood project's engineer talked about the drainage pond that would catch the runoff from hillsides and be stocked with fish. He talked about two community parks. The eventual build-out of more than nine hundred houses would be on 680 acres, including a hillside that Roy Ralph Breed says he will be looking at from his place instead of the ridgeline now filled with trees.

Standing on a dry patch of limestone in the middle of Barton Creek, Amelia says she knows there is little that can be done to stop development from eventually surrounding her and her sisters' land. She says she even gets offers from people who want her to sell off just two acres of her land so they can build a house. "I tell them no; who gets to do that when we struggled to buy all of our land in the country?"

Pure Luck is one of the very few working farms and ranches remaining on Barton Creek, which was settled from its end in Austin to its source out here by 1800s pioneers who grew crops and raised cattle or goats. It's a good thing that some people still can make a living today from the hardscrabble soil and the droughts-to-floods cycles of Central Texas. They are among the best and most-determined stewards of the land. They want to protect the water and soil that nourish their plantings and their animals. They want to see the creek and its tributaries run clear and clean. They want a future on their land for the next generation.

At the Dripping Springs council meeting with the Westwood developers and Amelia's neighbors up and down the creek, the longtime residents asked that the city take more time to consider its options. The response from the council was that the developers had done everything asked of them. "It's just going to keep happening," Amelia says as we walk back through the farm fields terraced long ago to keep erosion at bay. "I hope they all eat cheese."

I laugh with her at that summary of the inevitability of some development near her part of Barton

A large development planned nearby won't disrupt these happy goats.

Creek. It is going to happen, but I'm guardedly optimistic that land- and water-conservation measures will continue to make a difference in the western reaches of the creek's watershed. Landowners can choose easements over sellouts if local officials, voters, and land trusts fund that option. Developers can be brought to the table for settlements to put in better runoff and wastewater controls. If long-distance pipelines can be stopped, water from surface and ground sources increasingly will be a limitation on runaway growth. The future of Barton and other creeks, the watersheds, and the Edwards Aquifer—a natural bounty and lifeblood that makes Central Texas such a great place to live—is in our hands and our hearts.

FURTHER READING AND RESOURCES

Further Reading

Allan, J. David, and Maria M. Castillo. *Stream Ecology—Structure and Function of Running Water*s. New York: Springer, 2007.

Barnes, Michael. *Indelible Austin*. Austin: Waterloo Press, 2017.

———. *Indelible Austin—More Selected Histories*. Austin: Waterloo Press, 2018.

Beatley, Timothy. *Habitat Conservation Planning: Endangered Species and Urban Growth*. Austin: University of Texas Press, 1996.

Beletsky, Les. *Bird Songs Bible*. San Francisco: Chronicle Books, 2010.

Bones, James C., Jr., and John Graves. Texas Heartland: A Hill Country Year. College Station: Texas A&M University Press, 1975.

Brewer, Richard. Conservancy: The Land Trust Movement in America. Lebanon, NH: Dartmouth College Press, 2004.

Campbell, Linda. Endangered and Threatened Animals of Texas. Austin: Texas Parks & Wildlife Department, 2003.

Chapman, Brian R., and Eric G. Bolen. The Natural History of Texas. College Station: Texas A&M University Press, 2018.

Davis, Steven L. J. Frank Dobie: A Liberated Mind. Austin: University of Texas Press, 2009.

Doub, J. Peyton. The Endangered Species Act: History, Implementation, Successes and Controversies. Boca Raton, FL: CRC Press, 2012.

Estaville, Lawrence E., and Richard A. Earl. Texas Water Atlas. College Station: Texas A&M University Press, 2008.

Ferguson, Wes. The Blanco River. College Station: Texas A&M University Press, 2017.

Giller, Geoffrey. "A Fragile Balance." bioGraphic, California Academy of Sciences, January 24, 2017. https://www.biographic.com/posts/sto/a-fragile-balance.

Hardy, Thomas B., and Nicole A. Davis. Texas Riparian Areas. College Station: Texas A&M University Press, 2015.

Hynes, H. B. N. The Ecology of Running Waters. Caldwell, NJ: Blackburn Press, 2001.

Kimmel, Jim. The San Marcos: A River's Story. College Station: Texas A&M University Press, 2006.

Kramer, Ken, and Charles Kruvan. The Living Waters of Texas. College Station: Texas A&M University Press, 2010.

Lasley, Greg. Greg Lasley's Texas Wildlife Portraits. College Station: Texas A&M University Press, 2008.

Nelson, Willie, with Bud Shrake. Willie: An Autobiography. New York: Simon and Schuster, 1988.

Patoski, Joe Nick. Generations on the Land. College Station: Texas A&M University Press, 2010.

Perkins, Elaine. Hill County Paradise? Travis County and Its Early Settlers. Bloomington, IN: iUniverse, 2012.

Petranka, J. W. Salamanders of the United States and Canada. Washington, DC: Smithsonian Institution Press, 1998.

Pipkin, Turk, and Marshall Frech. Barton Springs Eternal. Austin: Softshoe Publishing, 1993.

Porter, Charles R., Jr. Sharing the Common Pool: Water Rights in the Everyday Lives of Texans. College Station: Texas A&M University Press, 2014.

Powell, Robert, Roger Conant, and Joseph T. Collins. Peterson Field Guide to Reptiles and Amphibians of

Eastern and Central North America. Boston: Houghton Mifflin Harcourt, 2016.

Pulich, Warren M. The Golden-cheeked Warbler: A Biological Study. Austin: Texas Parks & Wildlife Department, 1976.

Sansom, Andrew. Water in Texas: An Introduction. Austin: University of Texas Press, 2008.

Swearingen, William Scott, Jr. Environmental City. Austin: University of Texas Press, 2010.

Todd, David, and Jonathan Ogren. The Texas Landscape Project. College Station: Texas A&M University Press, 2016.

Weber, Lynne, and Jim Weber. Nature Watch Austin: Guide to the Seasons in an Urban Wildland. College Station: Texas A&M University Press, 2011.

Wood, Eric M., and Jherime L. Kellermann. Phenological Synchrony and Bird Migration: Changing Climate and Seasonal Resources in North America. Boca Raton, FL: CRC Press, 2017.

Resources

Austin Sierra Club: https://www.sierraclub.org/texas/austin

Balcones Canyonlands National Wildlife Refuge: https://www.fws.gov/refuge/balcones_canyonlands

Balcones Canyonlands Preserve: http://www.austintexas.gov/bcp

Barton Creek Habitat Preserve—The Nature Conservancy: https://www.nature.org/ourinitiatives/regions/northamerica/unitedstates/texas/placeswe-protect/barton-creek-habitat-preserve.xml

Barton Springs Conservancy: https://bartonspringsconservancy.org

Barton Springs Edwards Aquifer Conservation District: bseacd.org

Barton Springs University: http://bartonspringsuniversity.org

Clean Water Action: https://www.cleanwateraction.org/states/texas

Dobie-Paisano Fellowship University of Texas at Austin: https://dobiepaisano.utexas.edu/

Environmental Defense Fund: https://www.edf.org/offices/austin-texas

Hamilton Pool Road Matters: hprmatters.com

Hays County Historical Commission: www.hayshistoricalcommission.com/index.html

Hays Trinity Groundwater Conservation District: haysgroundwater.com

Hill Country Alliance: www.hillcountryalliance.org

Hill Country Conservancy: https://hillcountryconservancy.org

Meadows Center for Water and the Environment: www.meadowscenter.txstate.edu

National Wildlife Federation: https://www.nwf.org/southcentral

The Nature Conservancy—Texas: https://www.nature.org/ourinitiatives/regions/northamerica/unitedstates/texas/index.htm

No Dripping Sewage: https://nodrippingsewage.org

Protect Our Water: https://www.protectourwater.org

Save Barton Creek Association: http://www.savebartoncreek.org

Save Our Springs Alliance: https://www.sosalliance.org

Shield Ranch El Ranchito and Conservation Corps: https://www.elranchito.org/

Sierra Club Lone Star Chapter: https://www.sierraclub.org/texas

Texas Commission on Environmental Quality: https://www.tceq.texas.gov

Texas Conservation Corps American Youthworks: http://americanyouthworks.org/programs/texas-conservation-corps

Texas Land Trust Council: www.texaslandtrustcouncil.org

Texas Living Waters Project: http://texaslivingwaters.org

Travis Audubon Society: https://travisaudubon.org

Watershed Protection Department City of Austin: http://www.austintexas.gov/department/watershed-protection

INDEX

A Hill Country Paradise, 70
aboriculture, 12
Adams, Michael, 66–70
agarita, 45, 97
Alexander, Pleasant and Elizabeth, 32, 107
algae, 12, 16, 35, 39, 48, 83–92
Anarene, 90
Ann and Roy Butler Hike-and-Bike Trail, 6
archaeology, 27–28
Arrowhead Ranch, 111
arthropods, 15–16, 19
artifacts, 8, 24, 27–28, 101, 109
Audubon Society, 36, 75, 78
Austin Chamber of Commerce, 40
Austin City Council, 3, 7, 34, 58, 81
Austin Environmental Council, 36
Austin History Center, 10
Austin Nature & Science Center, 17
Austin Zoo, 66
Ayres, Atlee B., 49
Ayres, Patricia Anne Shield, 44–45, 49, 53–54
Ayres, Robert (Bob) Atlee, 44–53, 98, 102
Ayres, Robert M. Jr., 49

Babbitt, Bruce, 42
Balcones Canyonlands Conservation Plan (BCCP), 38, 58–59, 75
Balcones Canyonlands National Wildlife Refuge, 59–60, 73, 75
Balcones Canyonlands Preserve, 74, 79
bacteria, 3, 37, 39, 83–92
Ballew, Helen, 36, 48, 59
Barking Springs, 3

Barnes, Ben, 35
Barnett, Howard and Dorothy, 6
Barton Creek Country Club, 26, 35–37
Barton Creek Greenbelt, 10, 16, 38, 55–64, 72, 77
Barton Creek Habitat Preserve (BCHP), 14, 40, 48, 70–72, 74, 79–82, 110
Barton Creek Planned Unit Development (PUD), 34–35, 37, 41, 81
Barton Creek Square Mall, 26
Barton Creek watershed, 1, 38, 40, 43, 84, 86, 90, 110, 112
Barton Creek Wilderness Park, 15, 38, 48, 55–64
Barton: Eliza, 9; Parthenia, 9; William, 7–9; Zenobia, 9
Barton Hills, 1, 61
Barton Springs Bathhouse, 9–10
Barton Springs Conservancy, 10
Barton Springs Edwards Aquifer Conservation District, 92
Barton Springs Pool, 1–3, 5, 11; Eliza Spring, 8–9, 19–21; Main Spring, 9, 12, 21–22; Sunken Garden, 3, 9, 17–18, 20–21; Upper Spring, 9
Barton Springs Road, 6
Barton Springs University, 41–42
Barton Springs Uprising, 34–38, 58
Bassett, J. Marie, 32
Batts, Robert Lynn, 95, 97–98
Bear Creek, 43
Bear Creek watershed, 84
Bedichek, Roy, 10, 68
Bee Cave, 1, 14, 25, 43–44, 65–66, 70, 89, 92, 102
Bee Creek watershed, 74
Bendik, Nathan 19, 22–23

Berry, Wendell, 93–94
Bird, Sarah, 68
black-capped vireo, 46, 52, 60, 71, 73–82
Blanco River, 105
Bleakley, Anne Shahan, 111
Bleakley, Jack, 109–10
Bleakley, Marion Kingsberry, 111
Bleakley, Mark, 111
Blue Hole, 45, 54
Bohls, Dietrich, 70
Bohls, Gus, 70
Bolton, Claire, 117
Bolton, Denny, 117
Bolton, Hope, 117
Bowen, Marshall, 44–46
Bowen, Vera Ayres, 44–45, 49, 53
Boy Scouts, Capital Area Council, 89
Breed, Allene and Truman, Sr., 31–32
Breed and Company, 32
Breed, Benny, 31–32
Breed, Greg, 32–33
Breed, Roy Ralph and Connie, 113–16, 118
Breed, Terry, 116
Breed, Truman, Jr., 27, 31–33
Breed, Wanda, 31–32
Brooks, Harrison, 94–96, 98, 100
Brooks, Henry, 24, 93–100
Brooks, Kay, 94
Brooks, Victor L., 97–99
brown-headed cowbird, 77–78
Buda, 53, 92
Bull Creek, 36
Bullard, W. H., 62
Bunch, Bill, 35–38, 40, 43, 89, 91
Bunker Ranch, 111

Bush, George P., 78
Bush, George W., 39, 42
Butts, David, 38

Cabin on Barton Creek, 30
Camp Ben McCulloch, 16
Camp Wood Ranch, 46
Campbell's Hole, 55, 64
cattle, 9, 24, 45, 95–96, 101, 104, 113–115
cedar trees (Ashe juniper), 32–33, 76, 79, 93, 96–97
Chalk Knob Hollow, 49
Chamberlain, Dee Ann, 17–19, 23
Chapman, Don, 25
Cherry Canyon Ranch, 46
Chippindale, Paul, 18, 42
Circle C subdivision, 41
Citizens for a Barton Creek Park, 58
Citizens for Open Space, 58
Clamann, Andrew, 84, 86
Clean Water Act, 43
Clean Water Action, 36, 38
ClubCorp, 37
Cofer, George, 41–42, 59, 89
Collins School on Barton Creek, 32
Colorado River, 1–8, 44, 53, 73, 75, 107, 113–14
Combs, Susan, 78
Comprehensive Watershed Ordinance, 35, 37
Connally, John, 35
conservation easements, 39–40, 44–54, 75, 92, 94, 98, 101–12
Cooke, Lee, 34
Coupal, Ruben, 50
cousa, 116
Crawford, Brandon, 71–72, 79–82
Creasy, Mark, 57
Crooked Oak Cave, 92
Crow, Travis, 24–26, 90, 92, 94
Cuba, Nan, 65–67
cubic feet per second (CFS) flow rate, 6, 57

Dalrymple, Travis, 29–30
Davenport Ranch, 77
Davis, Frank, 98, 102–04, 107–11
Dedman, Robert H., 37
Deep Eddy Pool, 114
Deer Creek Ranch, 101
densiometer, 85
Devitt, Tom, 14–16, 23
Dobie, J. Frank, 10, 25, 65–69
Doerr, Doug and Kiff, 2, 105–09, 112
Donelson, Sarah, 83, 85
Driftwood, 92
Dripping Springs, 16, 24, 28, 43–44, 84, 89–90, 92–93, 106, 111, 118
Dripping Springs Conservation Design Ordinance, 112
Dripping Springs Water Supply Corporation, 90, 92
Dunn, Thomas, 97–98
Durrett, Leah, 56–57
dye test, 91
Dyne, Mark Van, 24–26

Earth Camp, 83
Earth First, 36
Eckols, Horace and Lola, 45
Edwards Aquifer, 1–3, 14, 16–18, 34–35, 38, 41–42, 84, 89, 97, 114, 119
El Buen Samaritano Episcopal Mission, 49
El Ranchito conservation camps, 49–51
Elks Club, 9, 19
Emma Long Park, 77
Endangered Species Act, 16–17, 42, 74–75
English, Randy, 80, 82
Environmental City, 36
Environmental Integrity Index (EII), 84–92
Environmental Protection Agency, 90
Estates of Barton Creek, 35, 41

Far Hills Ranch, 109–11
Farley, John, 111

fish, 5, 9, 12, 54
Fitzhugh Creek, 98
FM Properties, 35, 40
Francell, Jeff, 45, 98, 110
Freehold Communities, Inc., 89
Freeport-McMoRan, 35, 37, 41

Gaines Ranch, 58, 60
goats, 24, 31–32, 95–96, 101, 114–19
Goodacre, Glenna, 68
golden-cheeked warbler, 35, 39, 52, 60, 71, 73–79
graffiti, 40, 63–64
grasses: big bluestem, 97, 106; gamagrass, 97; Indian, 97, 106; King Ranch bluestem, 52, 97, 80; little bluestem, 76, 80, 97, 80, 106
Greene, A. C., 68
Griffith, Beverly, 59
Gully, Caroline Breed, 116
Gus Fruh Pool, 55, 62

Haas, Fred, 51
Hamilton Pool Road Matters, 52
Hancock, Clark, 41
Hand, Melissa, 64
Hatchett, John, 102–03
Hays County Commissioners Court, 107
Hays County Historical Commission, 32
Hazy Hills Ranch, 25, 89
Headwaters, 25, 88–90
Heath, Sandra, 64
Henry, Stuart, 36
Hernandez-Garay, Hansel Rene, 56
Herrington, Chris, 83–85
Hightower, Jim, 41
Hill Country Conservancy, 40–41, 62, 89, 92, 98, 102–03, 107–11
Hill Country Foundation, 36
Hill of Life, 56, 60
Hillis, David, 18, 42
Hillside at Spanish Oaks, 70

Hillwood Communities, 101
Hollon, Andy, 24–26
Hutchison, Vic, 42

invertebrates, 20, 86–87

Jackson, Todd, 83, 85, 87
Johns, David, 87–89, 92
Johnson, Lady Bird, 6
Johnson, Lyndon B., 6, 21

Kainz, Ceazar, 56
Kocher, Karen, 13
KUT, 37
Kuykendall, Marshall E., 39

Lady Bird Johnson Wildflower Center, 62
Lady Bird Lake, 6, 16
Lake Austin watershed, 74
Lakeway, 53, 102
Lasley, Greg, 75
Liberty Lunch, 34
Librach, Austan, 35
Little Barton Creek, 25, 52, 69–70, 86, 89, 102
Little Bear Creek watershed, 84
Little Fitzhugh Creek, 98
Living Springs documentary series, 13
Lone Star Land Steward Award, 48
Long Branch creek, 46
Longhorn Dam, 6
Lost Creek, 57, 60–62, 64, 87, 89
Lost Creek Municipal Utility District, 61
Lou Neff Point, 7–8
Lower Colorado River Authority (LCRA), 43, 89, 90
Lucas, Henry Lee, 66

Magellan Pipeline Company, 98
Mariposa Spring, 95, 98
Martinez, Alberto, 15, 44, 53, 64, 74, 115
May, Tip, 98–99
Meredith, Jim, 52, 102

Merz, Dalton, 96–97
Mockford, Phil, 67
Moffett, Jim Bob, 35, 37, 41
Moore, Enoch, 107
Moore, Lorenzo Daw, 106–08
Moore, Polly, 106–07
mop heads, 14–15, 21
Murden, Blake, 46, 49
Muse, Christy, 48, 53

National Environmental Policy Act, 79
Native Americans, 2, 8, 28, 71, 101, 109; Comanches, 8, 107; Lipan Apaches, 8; Tonkawas, 8
Natural Resources Conservation Service (NRCS), 96, 99, 103
Nature Conservancy, The, 14, 26, 36, 40, 45–48, 66, 70, 72, 79–81, 98, 110
Nelson, Willie, 25
Nissen, Brad, 14–16, 23

O'Donnell, Lisa and Jim, 74–79
Oliver, Bill, 43
Onion Creek, 2, 13–14, 16, 39, 43, 90–92, 111
Onion Creek Management Unit, 39
Onion Creek watershed, 43, 62, 84, 90, 92, 112
Outer Loop highway proposal, 53
Outstanding National Resource Water, 39

Paggi, Michael, 9
Paggi's Grist Mill, 9
Paisano Ranch, 65–70
Perkins, Alice Puryear, 103
Perkins, Elaine, 70
Perot, Ross, Jr., 101
Pogue, Alan, 34
Preserve at Barton Creek, 70, 81
Price, Andrew, 42
prickly pear cactus, 14–15, 69, 97, 108
Private Real Property Rights Preservation Act, 39

property rights, 26, 39
Protect Our Water, 90
Provence development, 52–53, 102
Pure Luck Farm and Dairy, 116–19
Puryear, Gary and Jennifer, 98, 100–04
Puryear, James, 100
Puryear, Thomas, 99

Rabb family, 9
Rathgeber, Dick, 89–90
Rathgeber Wilderness Scout Camp, 90
Real Estate Council of Austin, 40
Redford, Robert, 41, 93
Regional Water Quality Plan, 99
Reiner, Bill, 74, 76
Resolution Trust Corporation, 75
Resurrection Episcopal Church, 62, 64
Richards, Ann, 38–39
Robinson, Donelle, 19–22
Rocky Creek, 46, 50–51, 98, 100–01, 104
Rocky Creek development, 52, 91, 101–04
runoff, 1, 38–39, 43, 70, 76, 86–92, 97, 118–19

salamanders, 2–3, 10–14, 22, 42, 78, 89, 115: Austin blind salamander, 16–17, 16–18, 21, 42; Barton Springs salamander, 13–14, 16–18, 21, 39, 42, 99; breeding facility, 17–19, 23; Eliza daylighting project, 20; Jollyville Plateau salamander, 17; red salamander 19; San Marcos salamander, 17; Texas blind salamander, 17
Salinas, Mark, 63
San Marcos River, 105
Save Barton Creek Association (SBCA), 6, 36, 42–43, 58, 89
Schoolhouse Creek, 31
Scoggins, Mateo, 83, 85
sculpture, 7, 10, 68
Sculpture Falls, 56, 59–60
Sedwick, Shannon, 36
Sellstrom, Jean Quist family, 107

sewage, 16, 35, 43, 60–61, 86, 88, 90, 92
Shea, Brigid, 38
Sheffield, Beverly, 10, 58
Shield-Ayres Foundation, 49
Shield, Fred W. and Vera, 45
Shield Ranch, 15, 25, 44–54, 84–86, 98, 102–04, 110
Shield Ranch Foundation, 49
Shoal Creek, 7, 60
Shoal Creek Conservancy, 60
Sierra Club, 6, 36
Siff, Ted, 58–60
Slaughter Creek watershed, 84
Soil Conservation Service, 96
sonde, 85
SOS Alliance (Save Our Springs), 6, 36, 38, 41–43, 53, 89, 91
SOS Defense Fund, 38
SOS Ordinance, 16, 38, 40, 48, 58
Spanish explorers, 8
Spanish Oaks, 66, 69–70, 86
Splash exhibit, 10
Sports Country Camp, 24, 28–30, 84
St. Edward's University, 36, 74
Stark, Richard, Jr., 24–31
Stark, Richard Sr. and Susan, 24–31, 84
Stillwell, Cassidy, 56
streams, parts of, 84
SunCal, 112
Sunset Canyon, 89
Sunset Valley, 62
Swearingen, William S. Jr., 36
Sweethardt, Amelia, 116–18
Sweethardt, Gitana, 117
Sweetser, Sara, 116–17
Szilagyi, Pete, 109–110

Take Back Texas, 39
Texans for Positive Economic Policy, 78
Texas A&M University, 46, 52

Texas Agricultural Land Trust, 46
Texas Capitol Building, 8, 39
Texas Commission on Environmental Quality, (TCEQ), 52, 60, 90–91
Texas Conservation Corps, 64
Texas General Land Office, 78
Texas legislature, 34, 38–40, 48, 84
Texas Parks and Wildlife Department, 48, 79, 95, 103
Texas Public Policy Foundation, 78
Texas Supreme Court, 40
Tom Miller Dam, 6
Town Lake Beautification Committee, 7
Townes, John C., 89
Travis Country, 15
Trinity Aquifer, 89
Trinity University, 52
Tweedie, Reverend Billy, 62, 64
Twin Falls, 56, 60, 63

Unforeseen, The, 41, 93
University of Texas, 13, 16, 18, 25, 42, 57, 66, 68, 70, 87, 94, 97, 109, 111
University of Texas Environmental Science Institute, 42
University of Texas Tower, 8
Uplands, the, 70
Uplands Water Treatment Plant, 43, 89
US Department of Agriculture, 76, 98
US Department of the Interior, 79
US Fish and Wildlife Service, 16, 39, 42, 74, 78–79, 99
US Geological Survey, 43, 57, 82

Vickery, Paul, 50
Violet Crown Trail, 62
Vireo Hill, 82
Vireo Preserve, 73

Wagner, Staryn, 83–84
Walburg Store, 51
Waller Creek, 7
Walnut Springs Creek, 91
Water Utility Department, City of Austin's, 78, 92
Waterloo, 8, 16
Watershed Protection Department, City of Austin's, 14, 52, 78, 83–84, 86, 92
Waterway Restriction Guide, City of Austin's, 57
Watson, Kirk, 40
We Care Austin, 36
Webb, Walter Prescott, 10, 68
Weigel, Jeff, 48
West Travis County Public Utility Agency (WTCPUA), 52, 89
Westcave Outdoor Learning Center, 49–50
Westwood development, 112, 118
White, Thomas, 56
Wilcox, Thomas, 18
Wild Basin, 74
Williamson Creek watershed, 84
Wood River Massacre, 107

Yarnold, David, 78
Yznaga, Mark, 38

Zepeda, Nancy, 50
Zilker, Andrew Jackson, 9
Zilker Park, 2–3, 9–10, 55, 58, 63–64, 114; Zilker Park Boat Rentals, 6; Zilker Zephyr, 6
Zilker Park Posse, 36
Zilkr on the Park, 6